What goes on the title page?
The title, the author, the publisher, and the city like so:

PUBLISHING BASICS

Navigating the Self-Publishing Minefield

Robert Bowie Johnson, Jr. with Ron Pramschufer

Self Publishing, Inc., New York

In cooperation with Solving Light Books, Maryland

Where does the copyright page appear, and what's on it?

The copyright page is usually found on the back of the title page. We have the copyright notice, which includes the word "copyright," the symbol ©, the year, and the authors' names. You don't need both the word "copyright" and the symbol. Either will do, but just about every publisher uses both.

We have the publisher's name and address. We have the Library of Congress Catalog Number (LCCN), which is not required, and the International Standard Book Number (ISBN). We tell you where this book was printed. It is always a good idea to give credit to the printer and the designer as well.

Production Note: This book was printed on offset equipment and 50# recycled offset paper, and is a sample of that process (print runs of 500 or more). For samples of books printed on digital equipment (print runs of under 500 copies) or other paper stocks, contact your book coach or ron@rjcom.com.

How is this book organized to help me understand the self-publishing process?

We answer the most frequently asked questions (FAQs) about self-publishing and we steer you in the right direction. If, after reading this book, you have additional questions, please submit them directly through the *SelfPublishing.com* Web site.

Now and then we drop in a vivifying touch of humor to make sure that a stale groove doesn't trap the spinning wheels of your creative mind. Publishing your own books should be exciting and fun!

Contents

Is this the Acknowledgments page?

Yes, it is. While you are writing your books, keep a special folder or electronic file to make note of the people and organizations that help you. If you don't do this, you will most likely forget some very important people. You can't go wrong giving credit where credit is due. The people who help you write your books are your allies in your books' promotions.

I want to thank everyone who has asked me a question about self-publishing, and all those who have helped me frame the answers to those questions.

Is this the Dedication page?

Yes, and I dedicate this work to the memory of Erwin Knoll (July 17, 1931–November 2, 1994), former editor of *The Progressive* magazine, who taught me how to write and inspired me to be a writer. Teachers such as he are rare.

Publisher's Note to the Fourth Edition

The year 2000 marked the initial printing of *Publishing Basics: A Guide for the Small Press and Independent Self-Publisher*. Over twenty-five thousand copies have been distributed to a wide variety of writers, poets and independent publishers. Since that date, Self Publising, Inc., with its various Web sites, including *BooksJustBooks.com, SelfPublishing.com and RJCom.com,* has helped thousands of individual authors become publishers and print and sell over 100 million copies of thousands of titles ranging from personal memoirs to inspirational self-help books to illustrated children's books to urban fiction.

January 2009 is a time of great worldwide financial and political unrest. How it's all going to turn out is yet to be seen. The one thing, for sure, is that true self-publishing represents, not only a chance to express yourself but a genuine shot at the American dream of self-sustaining independence. Take the time to do it right. Don't fall for any of the "too good to be true" publishing schemes that permeate the Internet. Writing is a love and publishing is a business. If you understand this simple concept, you are well on your way to becoming a successful publisher. There is never a bad time to publish a good book. People read books in even the worst economic times.

If you haven't done so already, be sure to go to *www.PublishingBasics.com* and subscribe to the Publishing Basics Newsletter. The newsletter, with a circulation of over 60,000, serves as a monthly update to the Publishing Basics book. Good luck. Hope to see you soon.

—Ron Pramschufer,
January 2009

INTRODUCTION

While the printing process has changed dramatically over the past twenty years, the process of buying and selling printing has not changed much at all over the last hundred. The large conglomerate book printers print for the large conglomerate publishers. The second-tier book printers crave work from the same publishers that do business with the larger printers. They send their salesmen out to attract what they call "quality" publishers, ones that produce fifty to one hundred titles per year.

So where does that leave the small press and independent self-publishers? Too often they start out by taking their business to a smaller commercial printer that is not geared up for book production, but will at least make them feel like valued customers. The problem is that the cost is two or three times what is needed to compete effectively in the book marketplace.

Some self-publishers are able to find an actual book manufacturer out of the fifty thousand or so printers in the United States, but this generally doesn't work out much better. They wind up paying a significant premium because the marketing plans of these printers do not include small publishing companies or self-publishers.

Why don't these book printers want to deal with self-publishers? Here are some of the reasons printers have shared with me:

"They [self-publishers] aren't sure what they want."
"They take up too much of the estimator's time."
"They don't understand the printing process."
"They don't bring us their work in the right format."
"Our sales associates spend too much time with them."
"Getting paid on a timely basis is often a problem."

What it boils down to is that you, the self-publisher, represent an account that takes too much time and energy to service for the small amount of printing you buy. The printers want consistency and repeat business, and that's something that you, operating on your own, can't give them.

Enter *SelfPublishing.com*. Instead of your being one customer with one book, we combine you with hundreds of other customers and buy on your behalf, as a single, unified customer. The key is standardization. Much like Goodyear Tire, *SelfPublishing.com* offers a limited number of sizes in a limited number of styles—"tires off the rack," so to speak. One result of this standardization of product is that *SelfPublishing.com* buys at a significant discount and passes most of the savings on to you.

And our way of doing business solves all of the book printers' objections. First, because of our instant pricing function at the Web site, *SelfPublishing.com* jobs do not take up a minute of an estimator's time. *SelfPublishing.com* customers can still make all the specification changes they want, but they do it themselves at *SelfPublishing.com* the Web site. Second, *SelfPublishing.com* handles all the customer contact, so the printer deals with one experienced *SelfPublishing.com* person for dozens of books at any one time. Third, working with *SelfPublishing. com* ensures that all customer-furnished copy fits the printer's format.

Any problems with files or artwork are sorted out and corrected long before they get to the printer. Fourth, there is no sales associate and therefore no sales expense. We don't think you need to be sold anything. And finally, *SelfPublishing.com* customers pay in full for all their books by cash or credit card before they are shipped, so the printers, in turn, are happy to be paid promptly.

As an added bonus, *SelfPublishing.com* is not tied to any one technology. Our printer network includes digital printing houses, long- and short-run sheetfed printers, and web printers. These printers can efficiently handle anything from one hundred copies to one hundred thousand.

We treat all customers with respect, recognizing that you are the one hiring us to work for you. The same aggressive pricing applies to all customers equally.

We have designed this book to be an extremely useful resource for you. Please enjoy it, and good luck with all of your publishing projects. If you have additional questions, suggestions, or comments you'd like to share, please submit them directly to us at *SelfPublishing.com*.

—Ron Pramschufer

GENERAL QUESTIONS

How difficult is it to publish my own book?

You can do it easily and do it well with the help provided here. You have probably produced a flyer or handout at some time in your life. If so, you already have some self-publishing experience. Producing your completed book involves more work, of course, and you must overcome the inertia of just sitting there wishing you had a self-published book.

To exorcise the demon of the self-publishing doldrums, sing heartily to yourself. A song will spur and whip a lethargic mind to action. I'll even supply the words to your song:

> *Doubters and pessimists, come take a look!*
> *Yessirree, I'm going to publish my book.*
> *So dress me up and take me to the prom,*
> *Thanks for the help, SelfPublishing.com.*

Follow the advice on these pages and before long, your biggest problem just might be fending off the flunkies, flatterers, and parasites that dog the heels of the rich and famous.

What are some good reasons for self-publishing?

First, you don't have to convince anybody but yourself that your book should be published. Making a good case to yourself for the publication of a work you have created should not be difficult at all. No one else shares the high degree of enthusiasm you have for your book. Why give a third party, with intentions, interests, and priorities different from your own, the final say? Self-publishing gives you total control.

Second, if you have filled an existing void with your book and/or are able to create a demand for it, you will make more money than you would make with a standard publishing contract. Instead of a paltry 5% to 15% royalty, you'll make 20% to 80% of the purchase price. Once your self-published book is successful, you can negotiate with a larger publisher from a position of experience and strength.

Third, you can see your book in print within a few weeks, or at most, a few months, from the time you complete your manuscript. The larger publishers most often work on an eighteen month cycle, and that is just too long to wait.

Fourth, you can get distribution for your book through *Amazon.com* and *BarnesandNoble.com* just as easily as HarperCollins and Random House can for their books.

Fifth, you can preserve your own heritage—or that of your community, club, or whatever—in an inexpensive, quality format. Not everyone publishes to make a profit. Maybe you just want to leave a legacy with your family or share what you have learned with others.

Sixth, you can produce your book inexpensively through *SelfPublishing.com*.

Are you really a Self-publisher?

Self-publishing is made up of two words: *Self* which refers to you (self) in the first person and *Publishing* which implies there is a Publisher as in a publishing company. In order to be recognized as a publishing company by the book industry you need to own the International Standard Book Number (ISBN) that is listed in your book. *Nobody* can sell, give or assign you an ISBN except for R.R. Bowker, the North American ISBN agency. Unless you buy an ISBN directly from R.R. Bowker, or through one of their authorized agents, as listed on the R.R. Bowker Web site, you are not a publisher; therefore you are not a self-publisher. You might be an author who pays a Vanity Press to publish your book so you can call yourself a "Published Author," but you are not a self-publisher. The whole ISBN issue is dealt with in more detail further ahead in this book.

What qualifies you to write a book like this?

I'm qualified because I did it. Here it is. You are reading it. In the same way, you will become qualified to write and publish your book by doing it.

I have much writing, editing, and publishing experience behind me, which helps. If you don't have that kind of experience, you learn from the experience of others, and read books such as this to become qualified yourself. This book, in particular, leads you to (or back to) *SelfPublishing.com*, where you will find access to every resource you need to turn your publishing goal into a reality.

What is the story behind the development of this book?

I had self-published two books and was working on several more when a friend told me about the *SelfPublishing.com* Web site. I saw on the home page that I could get an instant price on a book. I had a 176-page book in my computer formatted for the economical 5.5 x 8.5 trim size. I clicked my mouse a few times, filled in some blanks, and within two minutes I had a price. It had taken me, on the average, more than a week to get higher estimates on the same book from different printers around the country. *SelfPublishing.com* impressed me with its range, efficiency, and professionalism.

I searched the rest of the Web site and ordered their free book on the fundamentals of publishing. It was a good book, but it hadn't really caught up with the speed and convenience of *SelfPublishing.com*. I e-mailed Ron Pramschufer, one of the principals of the company, and suggested that I do a concise self-publishing book for writers like you and me that would incorporate what *SelfPublishing.com* had to offer. Ron told me that he had been thinking about the same thing for a while, and we struck a deal. We agreed that we wanted to create a book that would complement the Web site. And here it is! Can't you now picture your own book beginning to make the transition from idea to reality?

What makes self-publishing an attractive option?

The old saying "The first copy of your book costs a whole lot, but they're pretty inexpensive after that" is as true today as it was a hundred years ago. The setup charges are the same no matter what the quantity. The higher the setup cost, the larger the print run needed to amortize these costs into an acceptable unit cost.

Today's technology has reduced these setup costs whether you are printing a black-and-white novel or a full-color coffee table book. As little as fifteen years ago, typesetting made up a major portion of a book project's setup costs. Then, a standard 6 x 9" page cost between $6 and $10 to typeset and proofread. A project requiring two or three rounds of galley proofs and a set or two of page proofs could easily run that cost up to $15 or $20 per page. That meant that a 256-page book would cost $4,000 to $5,000 before you even got to the printer, which would then have to shoot and strip negatives at a cost of perhaps $7,500.

Today, the $600 computer with basic word processing software and the advent of Portable Document Format (PDF) has replaced the type houses of old. The laser printer has replaced expensive photo paper and chemicals. New computer-to-plate (CTP) techniques bypass film completely. The average savings to the small publisher amount to as much as $6,500 per title.

As a result, writers can put their own books into publication cost-effectively in relatively low quantities.

Why won't bookworms eat the pages of cartoon books?
They taste funny.

Should I start my own publishing company?

Absolutely. With the publishing of your first book, your activities in that regard become a publishing operation. You might as well name it and get a PO Box. If you have a UPS store or something similar nearby, rent one of their boxes and your address will sound better: 1050 Pine Tree Boulevard, Suite 116, for example. Suite 116 at Mailboxes, Etc. is very, very small—but nobody will know that but you. You can even use your home address for your new publishing company. Just add "Suite 102" and the publishing giants will have nothing on you, address-wise.

You need a publishing company to get your International Standard Book Numbers (ISBNs) and Library of Congress Catalog Numbers (LCCNs) associated with you. You can purchase a single one or a block of ten ISBNs. Be determined to use most of them if not all. Your first book may be good, but it just might be your fifth or sixth book that becomes a blockbuster! Once you have the experience of publishing your own book under your belt, you can help other writers get published—through your company, using one of your ISBNs.

Beware of companies that assist self-publishers and claim to supply the ISBN and LCCN for your book for a small fee. These numbers will always be associated with them, not you!

Naming your company takes some thought. Don't be hokey, now! What do I mean by that? Naming my publishing company "Bob Johnson Publishing" would be hokey. Come up with a simple name that is easy to remember, is descriptive, and will not limit you in the future. If your first book is a children's book and you name your company "Child's Play Publishing," for example, you won't be able to add teenage and adult books to your list without changing the name. Once you have narrowed your choices, check these resources in the library to avoid company name duplication: *Small Press Record of Books, Publishers Directory* by Gale Research, and *Books in Print*. Actually, the most important consideration in choosing a company name is whether or not the URL (*www.yourname.com*) is available. To check availability, go to *e-moxie.com*.

The basic business structures are sole proprietorship, partnership, and corporation. Most first-time publishers choose the sole proprietorship because it's the easiest to form. In the end, your tax advisor or attorney will be able to help you determine which business structure is best for you.

What is the difference between a vanity press, a subsidy press, and a packager?

Linda and Jim Salisbury, the authors of *Smart Self-publishing*, define a subsidy press as "a publishing company that applies its ISBN to a book and charges the author for the cost of production. The author receives only a few copies of the book, and is promised royalties on those copies that might be sold by the subsidy press." They define a vanity press as "another term for a subsidy press. It implies that the published book has no value other than to stroke the author's ego." So a vanity press and a subsidy press are basically the same.

I responded to the ads for two subsidy presses in a national magazine and a week later received their introductory packets. Both of them were very slick and impressive—on the surface. I must commend the first one for its "Word of caution about financial returns." They write:

> No one can predict how a book will sell and, consequently, how much of your fee you are likely to regain by publishing your work with us. Some authors have received satisfactory returns. Others, however, did not find the market receptive and their financial rewards have been negligible. On the other hand, if financial success is not your prime concern, and if personal satisfaction ranks high in your desire for publication, then by all means consider our subsidy publishing program.

If you have money to burn and only want a few books, this may be the way to go. If you don't have money to burn, the subsidy press process will work something like this: step 1, send in your manuscript for evaluation; step 2, sign a contract for between $10,000 and $15,000;

step 3, go to the bank to get a second mortgage or use your 18% credit card to make the payment; step 4, get a few copies of your finished book; step 5, experience acute attacks of buyer's remorse while continuing to make payments on your mortgage or credit card for the next five or ten years. The second subsidy publisher was less up-front, but was pretty much the same story as the first.

A book packager acts as an independent contractor to bring a predetermined number of your books into being. All the books belong to you. Book packagers work for a pre-set fee, and all the profits are yours. When I showed off my self-published books at a writers' group meeting, one of the members asked me how I did it. She hired me to produce her book because she didn't want to be bothered with the details. Just like that, I was a book packager! You can do the same with your book(s). The people at *SelfPublishing.com* make it easy for you to become your own packager and publisher, saving thousands of dollars in the process.

What is a cooperative publisher?

A term that surfaces from time to time is a hybrid of a book packager and a subsidy publisher, called a cooperative publisher. Like the book packager, the author enters into a publishing agreement with the cooperative publisher to produce a fixed number of books for a fixed amount of dollars. When the printing is complete, a certain number of these books are the sole property of the author and the rest are used for joint marketing and sales. This agreement is for a fixed period of time during which, if the book sells out, the cooperative publisher will reprint the book at his expense. Royalties of 50% of net revenue on the initial printing are paid twice a year. As with the subsidy press, the author uses the cooperative publisher's ISBN number. The problem with this type of publisher is that 99% of the time it is simply a vanity publisher with a catchy new name.

What is *on-demand* book printing?

Since the days of Gutenberg, book printing has been *on-demand*. The publisher "demands" and the printer "prints." The implied meaning of the word is that you can order books, cost-effectively, one book at a time. While there are thousands of digital printers, there are only a few who can produce books in the implied manner.

Don't get all caught up with words. Printing is what it has always been—a combination of price, service, and quality. You normally can't get all three. It's up to you, as the publisher, to decide.

What are *on-demand* or POD book publishers?

A typical on-demand (POD) publisher sets up your digital manuscript to be printed one book at a time using a digital press. You pay a set fee of between $350 and $1,250 and receive in return one hard cover copy of your book and one paperback copy. If they set the retail price of the paperback at $18, say, then each additional book you order from them costs you $10.80 (40% off the retail price). If a bookstore, wholesaler, or on-line bookseller orders your book, you receive a royalty ranging from $1 to $2.30 per book. Think about it from a strictly business point of view. Every time you sell a book that you've paid for and published through *SelfPublishing.com*, you recoup the cost of that book and more—perhaps double or even triple the cost. The sale of a book through an on-demand publisher recoups only a small percentage of that book's cost for you. If you don't think you can sell any more than five or ten or twenty books of a new title, on-demand is the way to go. If you think you can sell at least a hundred books, you want to stick with *SelfPublishing.com*. On-demand printing also allows publishers to economically keep a book in print that may sell only a handful of copies per month after the book has run its course in the marketplace.

Additionally, while a handful of legitimate POD publishers do exist, most POD publishers are Vanity Press Publishers who charge authors a premium to publish their books.

What is a *book coach*, and how can one help me?

A *book coach* is a publishing consultant without the frills. A talented and dedicated book coach works closely with you to save you many hours of time, tons of frustration, and lots of money. As with everything else in the Internet publishing world, there are plenty of people out there waiting to pick your pocket. If you are going to hire a book coach, do your homework. Get references and in no case pay more than a couple hundred dollars for the service. *SelfPublishing.com* supplies a book coach to their customers. They are available to answer general questions at no charge.

What is e-publishing?

It is no secret that computers of all types are an integral part of nearly everyone's life. The idea of *e-publishing* has been the darling of a certain crowd since the early part of the decade. Tens of millions of venture capital dollars have been dumped into the concept that people have grown tired of reading paper bound books and will jump at the idea of staring at a computer screen to fill their reading needs. The first round of e-publishing died off the second the venture capital money ran out. Book people were book people—period.

The *e* concept is attractive for a variety of reasons, with the main one being that the production costs are pretty much non-existent. The idea of cutting the printer out of the picture is not new. The problem is getting the consumer on board and I just don't see it happening anytime soon. It's not that it doesn't work at all. You might be reading the e-version of the publishing basics book right now but I'll bet you a dozen donuts that if you are, you have printed out the PDF and are reading a pile of printed paper. Another situation perfect for e-books are study guides, such as Cliff's Notes. Picture yourself back in college on a Sunday night and you are just getting around to studying for a test in the morning. The bookstores are closed so the only way you can get your hands on the material is to go online and buy the e-book. But even in this example, couldn't the study guide people do just as well offering the same information for a fee, on their Web site? Absolutely.

The latest entry into the *black hole* money trap of e-publishing is Amazon with their Kindle reader. All of the press clippings would have you believe that every other person out there is shelling out $399 and reading their books on their Kindle. Actually, if you read in-between the lines a little on the latest press hype, all of the Kindle functions except for the reading of books are mentioned.

One last note on the subject until the fifth edition of the Publishing Basics book is published; I ride the train to and from work each day with four hundred thousand other commuters into New York City. I take an informal poll each day of who is doing what to entertain themselves during the hour commute. I have yet to see a single person with a Kindle doing anything, much less reading an e-book. How about you? Have you seen one? That's what I thought.

The race is not over and it's hard to say exactly how it will turn out, but for now my advice is to save your money. It's less clear than ever whether the e-book will be the next CD or MP3 or just another 8-track.

How do I get my work copyrighted?

The law grants you copyright protection automatically upon the creation of your work. Your work need not be completed to be protected. You own the copyright on your work as you create it. No publication or registration or other action in the US Copyright Office is required to secure copyright. There are, however, definite advantages to registration. Among these are the following:

- Registration establishes a public record of the copyright claim.
- Before an infringement suit may be filed in court, registration is necessary for works of US origin.
- If done before or within five years of publication, registration will establish prima facie evidence in court of the validity of the copyright and of the facts stated in the certificate.
- If registration is made within three months after publication of the work or prior to an infringement of the work, statutory

damages and attorney's fees will be available to the copyright owner in court actions. Otherwise, only an award of actual damages and profits is available to the copyright owner.

- Registration allows the owner of the copyright to record the registration with the US Customs Service for protection against the importation of infringing copies.

The copyright notice that appears in your published books should be similar to the one in this book. It should include the name of the copyright owner, the year of first publication, and the word *copyright* or the symbol ©. When the copyright notice appears, an infringer cannot claim that he or she did not realize the work was protected.

You, as author and copyright owner, are wise to place a copyright notice on any unpublished copies of your work, or portions thereof that leave your control.

The use of the copyright notice is your responsibility and does not require advance permission from, or registration with, the Copyright Office.

Your copyright lasts from the moment of your work's creation (when it first appears in tangible form) until seventy years after your death. The copyright for a work prepared jointly by two or more authors lasts for seventy years after the last surviving author's death.

How do I find the copyright symbol on my computer?

Every good word processor today gives you access to important characters that do not appear on the keyboard. They are called ANSI and ASCII character sets. To get the © character, make sure the Num Lock key on the right-hand side of your keyboard is on, and use those numbers for coding the character (the numbers at the top of the keyboard will not work). Now, hold down the Alt key and press 0169. When you release the Alt key, © will appear where your cursor is. From one writer to another, I am happy to present the access numbers to the following very useful set of characters hiding in your computer:

^	094	‰	0137	~	0126
•	0149	™	0153	œ	0156
¢	0162	©	0169	§	0167
£	0163	®	0174	µ	0181
¶	0182	±	0177	°	0176
1/4	0188	1/2	0189	3/4	0190
¿	0191	À	0192	Á	0193
Â	0194	Ã	0195	Ä	0196
Å	0197	Æ	0198	C	0199
È	0200	É	0201	Ê	0202
Ë	0203	Ì	0204	Í	0205
Î	0206	Ï	0207	x	0208
Ñ	0209	Ò	0210	Ó	0211
Ô	0212	Õ	0213	Ö	0214
Ø	0216	Ù	0217	Ú	0218
Û	0219	Ü	0220	x	0221
x	0222	ß	0223	à	0224
á	0225	â	0226	ã	0227
ä	0228	å	0229	æ	0230
ç	0231	è	0232	é	0233
ê	0234	ë	0235	ì	0236
í	0237	î	0238	ï	0239
x	0240	ñ	0241	ò	0242
ó	0243	ô	0244	õ	0245
ö	0246	÷	0247	ø	0248
ù	0249	ú	0250	û	0251
ü	0252	x	0253	x	0254

and my favorites: – (en dash) 0150 and — (em dash) 0151.

Since I've been using these symbols, I don't know how I ever got along without them. I'd feel especially lost without the em dash—I really would. And what a pleasure, instead of writing *resume,* to be really cool and write *résumé.*

On an older Mac, use key caps (under the apple) and press the Option key, the Command key, and the Shift key to find the character you want. If you're running System 10, it's a little trickier. In Panther, launch System Preferences and choose the International preference. Click the Input Menu tab and enable the Input Menu option. When you do so, the Show Input Menu in Menu Bar option is enabled and the Input menu appears in the Finder. To reveal the Keyboard Viewer window, just select Keyboard Viewer from the Input menu. (That's if you're not using one of the excellent font utility programs available— Font Reserve™ or Suitcase™.)

What is an International Standard Book Number (ISBN)?

The International Standard Book Number (ISBN) is a thirteen-digit number (it used to be ten-digits) that uniquely identifies books and book-like products published internationally. The purpose of the ISBN is to establish and identify one title or edition of a title from one specific publisher. The ISBN is unique to that edition, allowing for more efficient marketing of products by booksellers, libraries, universities, wholesalers, and distributors.

If you have established your own publishing company— basically, a name and an address to begin with—you can purchase ISBNs from R.R. Bowker, the US agency licensed to sell them. If you live outside the US, you need to visit the International ISBN Web site and find the agency assigned to your country. Numbers are sold in blocks, starting at 10. I generally recommend purchasing at least 10 if you are at all serious about entering the publishing business. Remember, you need to assign a separate number for every version of every title you produce. The ten numbers go pretty quickly. You'd be surprised.

The ISBN is printed on the copyright page of hard cover and paperback books, and on the lower portion of the back cover of a paperback book above the bar code. Some major publishers place the ISBN on the back cover of their hard cover books, and some don't. It really doesn't matter.

Let's say you have started a publishing company and published your first book, assigning to it the first of your ten ISBNs you purchased. Be sure that when you have finished copies of your book, that you go back to R.R. Bowker, the database of record of the ISBN Agency and do what is required to be listed in *Books in Print*. This is a very important directory used by many bookstores. And always be sure to put your ISBN on all your promotional literature.

Are there any legitimate single ISBN's available?

Single ISBN's are now available from either R.R. Bowker or one of a handful of authorized agents, including Self Publishing, Inc. The complete list of authorized agents is listed on the Bowker Web site. What is not listed is the fact that many of the authorized agents also offer authors a Vanity Press option. Unfortunately it is *Buyer Beware* on that one. To play it safe, I would purchase your single ISBN either directly from Bowker or through Self Publishing, Inc., at a pretty good discount. Self Publishing, Inc., does not offer a *vanity press* option so there is no way you can get confused.

Can't I have someone assign me one of their ISBNs?

No. The most common tactic used by today's vanity/subsidy presses is to tell you that they will *assign* or *sell* you an ISBN. They lead you to believe that your book is registered in your name and reinforce this by telling you "You retain all the rights." This is all double-talk. Nobody can give or assign you a number. They can let you use one of their numbers, but you do not own it. The orders for that book (ISBN) will always go to that publisher. If you change publishers (and I use that term loosely), the ISBN does not go with you; it remains theirs. You will need to start all over with your marketing efforts under your new ISBN number.

Do I really need my own ISBN?

Yes. The ISBN is what identifies you as the publisher. Once you have obtained your ISBNs from R.R. Bowker, you are no longer a *self-publisher*. You are a *publisher*—an independent publisher. There is no difference at that point between you and Random House except for the fact that Random House publishes more titles than you (more than most publishers, for that matter). You assign one of these numbers to your first book. Once you own the ISBN, it remains the same for the life of the book. You can change printers, distributors, wholesalers, retailers, or whatever else you want—the book remains yours. If, ten years from now, someone orders a copy of your book, you, as the publisher, will get the order. If you don't own the number, the person who does will get the order.

What about bar codes?

The ISBN for your book is easily translated into a globally compatible bar code format called a Bookland (European Article Number) EAN. Every bookstore chain and most smaller bookshops use bar code scanning at the checkout register. If you didn't know that, you haven't been to a bookstore in the last twenty years, and I'd say it's time for you to visit one.

Putting the bar code on your book is part of the book cover designer's job, and it's a simple one. Using a software program, the designer types in your ISBN, and the bar code comes up in just the right place on your back cover. You can put your book's retail price near the bar code on the back cover if you want to. That doesn't mean that retailers will always have to charge the full amount. Using their computers, they can tie your Bookland EAN code to a sale price, and that's what will appear on the register when your book is scanned.

If you are using a bar code, it must be black or a color dark enough to be scanned. Keep this in mind when counting the number of colors on your cover.

What about a Library of Congress Catalog Number?

It's a good idea to get one if you plan to sell your book to libraries, but you don't have to have it printed in the book itself (so it's OK if you do apply for it while your book is printing). All you have to do is apply for a Library of Congress (LC) Pre-Assigned Card Catalog Number (PCN). It doesn't cost anything and it can be ordered for any book over fifty pages (genealogies and children's books fewer than fifty pages are an exception to this rule). The Library of Congress Web site is www.loc.gov.

What are BISAC codes and where do I get them?

BISAC stands for Book Industry Standards and Communications. Sometimes referred to as a *Book Industry Subject and Category* code, BISAC codes are numbers assigned to books to more easily categorize them for retailers, distributors, and libraries. When you fill out the Books in Print form, you'll be asked for three BISAC codes that best describe your book's subject. Baker & Taylor, one of the major book distributors, also requires them if you register a title with them. You can review and choose BISAC codes at the Web site for the Book Industry Study Group: (www.bisg.org/standards/bisac_subject/major_subjects. html). If you're not sure which codes best fit your book, check out similar books at your bookstore or library and see which codes were chosen for them.

EDITORIAL QUESTIONS

Where can I get writing help?

All you have to do is search the internet for connections. There you will find all kinds of writing clubs and societies eager to help members improve their skills. I especially recommend these nine books:

- *On Writing Well,* by William Zinsser: An informal guide to writing nonfiction
- *If You Want to Write,* by Brenda Ueland: A book about art, independence, and spirit
- *The Writer's Chapbook,* edited from *Paris Review* interviews and with an introduction by George Plimpton: A compendium of fact, opinion, wit, and advice from the twentieth century's pre-eminent writers
- *The Elements of Editing,* by Arthur Plotnik: A modern guide for editors and journalists; Editing is writing.
- *Woe Is I,* by Patricia T. O'Conner: The grammarphobe's guide to better English in plain English
- *12 Keys to Writing Books That Sell,* by Kathleen Krull: A mirror that will help you see the strengths and weaknesses in your writing
- *Technique in Fiction,* by Robie Macauley and George Lanning: An imaginative rather than mechanical approach to a complicated subject, featuring a splendid variety of examples
- *The Writer's Digest Handbook of Novel Writing,* from the editors of *Writer's Digest*: Practical advice and instruction for creating a novel
- *100,000 Plus Power Phrases for Students, Writers, Speakers, and Business People,* by Robert Bowie Johnson, Jr.: A study of ideas and a stimulant to deep and original thinking

Whether you think you need writing help or not, I highly recommend that you subscribe to *Writer's Digest* magazine. They call their classifieds the "Writer's Mart," and it's worth the price of the subscription just to have access to that. There you can find writing classes, conferences, and contests; editing, critiquing, and ghostwriting services; and much more. When you get your *Writer's Digest* each month in the mail, you'll remember that you subscribe to it because you are a writer! It's easy to forget that sometimes, believe me.

Where should I go for critiquing help?

If you want to save money, try to get a qualified friend to help you. Perhaps you can find an English teacher or graduate student at a nearby college who would be willing to help in exchange for acknowledgement in your book. Members of local writers' groups often help each other with editing. Or, if you are willing to invest a small amount of money you can ask the professionals at *SelfPublishing.com* by purchasing an "Editorial Analysis."

Just what is an Editorial Analysis?

SelfPublishing.com's Editorial Analysis will provide you with a general evaluation of the following as well as a specific recommendation as to the level of editorial service they recommend for your manuscript (if any).

- Appropriateness of content for the intended readership
- General strengths and weaknesses of the manuscript relevant to engaging the target audience
- Structure and organization
- Likely effectiveness of writing style and level as it affects pacing and reader comprehension
- Writing mechanics and language usage issues involving grammar, syntax, punctuation, and spelling

- Permissions
- Documentation, bibliography, sourcing notes, references, and citations

Three different levels of editing are offered and may be recommended. They are mechanical, substantive and comprehensive.

Is an Editorial Analysis, really necessary? Why can't I just select my own editing service?

There is no reason you can't, as long as you find a truly neutral person to do the analysis. Your mom, or any other family member, would probably not be a good choice. Using a service that also provides the editorial services suggested is also a bit problematic, although this is what I do with *Selfpublishing.com*. Isn't that a little two-faced, you might be asking yourself. I thought so too, which is why the Editorial Analysis is set up as a stand-alone element with *SelfPublishing.com*. It is up to the author whether to use our analysis and then go to another editor or use someone else's analysis to determine the type of editing to buy from *SelfPublishing.com* or, most importantly, not to purchase any editorial service from *SelfPublishing.com* but still be able to use the design and printing services. I can say, though, in the half dozen years we have been offering this analysis, I have yet to have any real negative experience with the service.

Good: Your diligent editing uncovers 99 errors in your writing.
Bad: After it's published.

What is my role as the editor in the self-publishing process and what are my responsibilities?

As a self-publisher you are the publisher and wear every hat in your publishing organization. Just as Simon & Schuster can send a manuscript out to an outside person or service for editing, Simon & Schuster is responsible for what is published. When you hire an editor or editorial service, you are not waiving the responsibility for the content in your book. On the other hand, no editor or editorial service is going to accept that responsibility or liability. This is not meant to scare you but it is reality. I was never more than a B student in English so I am quite happy to have someone look at anything I write and I normally agree with the changes the editor recommends. But at the end of the day, if it goes out with my name on it, I am responsible for the final content—period. Don't take that responsibility lightly.

How involved does the editor get? Will the editor change my voice?

The editor gets involved in that he/she reads everything you have written, but your voice will not be changed. At *SelfPublishing.com*, all editing is conducted in a manner that preserves your voice, as the author, so the book is still really your own after editing. The editors work to clarify your intended meaning, and not to change the meaning of your content.

What level of editorial service do I need to purchase to ensure a completely error free manuscript?

Finding the answer to this question is right up there with trying to find the Holy Grail. The easy answer is, "no manuscript is ever perfect." I guess I can buy into that statement, at least conceptually, but I am still left with the follow-up question, "If no manuscript is perfect, exactly how imperfect is considered acceptable?" Whenever I ask that question, all the editor types tend to clear the room. Unfortunately there just doesn't seem to be a clear cut answer, which ends up leading right back to you, the publisher. Common sense tells you that there will be fewer errors after two editorial passes, than with one, especially if that second pass is a different person. It follows that even fewer errors will exist after three passes—four—five.... While this is true, you need to be realistic. Remember, you are running a business. The best thing to do is to keep your initial press run low enough so you see yourself coming back for a reprint within six months or so. Then simply keep track of any errors that may have slipped through and make the changes in the reprint. Meanwhile, if you find the editor who will guarantee a perfect edited manuscript, send them my way.

What if I, as the author do not like the recommendations made by the editor? Do I have to accept them?

No, you don't. Your word document will be returned to you with tracked changes and it is up to you to accept or delete each of them.

What is a Mechanical Edit?

The purpose of this level of editing is to prepare an already well structured manuscript for publication. A mechanical edit may address any of the following as needed:
- Correct errors in spelling
- Correct words that can be found easily in a dictionary or credible on-line resource
- Correct errors involving words that have similar spelling or sound such as:
  » *manager* and *manger*
  » *there, their,* and *they're*
  » *affect* and *effect*
  » *two, too,* and *two*
  » *it's* and *its*
  » *insure, ensure,* and *assure*

- Correct errors in possessives involving names, as well as both singular and plural possessives
- May query inconsistencies in specialty terms that are not commonly known by the public and are difficult to verify
- May query inconsistencies in names and places that are fictional or not well-known
- Correct errors in punctuation including:
  » Ellipses
  » Different types of dashes including en and em dashes
  » Hyphenations
  » Commas
  » Colons
  » Semicolon
  » Quotation marks
  » Apostrophes
  » Various punctuation marks within sentences and at the end of sentences
  » Sentence fragments
  » Run-on sentences
- Correct errors in grammar including:
  » Subject/verb agreement
  » Mixture of tenses
  » Issues involving plural and singular
  » Treatment of possessives
  » Basic syntax (the way in which words are put together to form phrases or sentences)
- Correct errors in capitalization
- Ensuring that proper capitalization rules are applied in different situations such as:
  » Titles of persons
  » Titles of various types of works
  » Specific terms including those referring to directions, seasons, and languages
- Identify some basic language usage issues such as:
  » Words that are used incorrectly as in: "Incontinence" when "incompetence" was intended

» Incorrect attempted use of a noun as a verb as in: "Impact" "Strategy" and "strategize"
- Suggest changes in word choice in cases when:
    » A word is overused
    » A different word choice may more clearly convey the meaning
    » Some readers may find a particular word offensive

What is a Substantive Edit?

This level of editing is recommended primarily for manuscripts needing attention to organization, presentation, and sentence structure to clarify meaning and smooth the flow of the text. Mechanical issues are addressed in the later copy edit stage. The substantive edit may address any of the following as needed.

- Suggest improvements to the organization and presentation of material to enhance the reader's experience with the content. This may include:
    » Recommendations for recasting tables, charts, or figures
    » Recommendations for adjusting the format used to present the material
    » Recommendations to add or delete sections of the manuscript
    » Recommendations to reorder some of the material
- Identify information that may need citations and/or permissions
- Check formatting of references cited
- Flag terms or phrases that may convey an unintended meaning, such as:
    » Bias
    » Negative or offensive tone
    » Alternative message or implication for some within the intended audience

- Identify inconsistencies or contradictions within the text, such as in:
  - » Concepts
  - » Characterization details
  - » Plot points
- Suggest more extensive rewording and restructuring of sentences to:
  - » Clarify meaning
  - » Tighten prose
  - » Smooth the flow of text

What is a Comprehensive Edit?

Our Comprehensive Editing Process is closet to the type of treatment it would receive if published by a major publisher, and recommended for manuscripts with a solid conceptual foundation that would benefit from more extensive structural, organizational, and developmental work. This edit provides recommendations for more substantial changes to improve the manuscript. Later stages of editing in this process provide more detailed assistance with the presentation of content as well as the writing mechanics.

Phase 1 - Sample Comprehensive Edit
- Editor reviews entire manuscript and creates a ten to fifteen page sample edit, and provides the author with a brief overview of the recommended structural and developmental changes.
- Author reviews sample edit to ensure the initial recommendations are consistent with his goals for the writing project.
- Author returns the sample edit, including any additional information or instructions for the editor.
- Author and editor hold a phone conference to discuss the focus of the edit with respect to the goals for the project.

Phase 2 - Comprehensive Editing
- Based on the sample edit and the phone conference, the editor continues providing structural, organizational, and

developmental recommendations throughout the manuscript and completes the Comprehensive Edit.

- Author reviews the edited manuscript, and revises the manuscript based on the editor's recommendations.
- Author returns the revised manuscript.

Phase 3 - Substantive Editing
See question about Substantive Editing

Phase 4 - Mechanical Editing
See question about Mechanical Editing

After I am all finished looking over what the editor gave me, how can I be sure there aren't any errors?

You can't really. No editor will find every error, that's just a fact of life. But, if you think another "set of eyes" would be a good idea, then order what *SelfPublishing.com* calls an *Additional Proofing Pass*. Regardless of the editorial service you may have already completed, once you have revised based on the edit, you may find yourself wanting an editor to see it again. Maybe you would like help to be sure you addressed all of the suggested edits, questions, and comments. Maybe it would be nice to get help to ensure you applied the changes accurately. Also, after having addressed many editing issues, what if there are now additional errors or concerns that would come to light, even though they were not apparent in the earlier edit, when there were so many more issues to be handled? You may notice that as the manuscript becomes cleaner, another editorial pass could help to fine-tune your manuscript and take it to an even higher level of quality before you send it to the design department.

Even after the design process, it may be a good idea to have another review by an editor experienced in preparing manuscripts for publication. Such an editor may catch errors that can and do occur as the manuscript is transformed into a book during the design and formatting process. An editor could review it for any formatting issues, dropped text, inconsistent fonts or margins, spacing, widows and orphans, and could also check for last minute problems with spelling and punctuation.

Although published books are never completely perfect, an additional editorial pass may be just what you need to boost your confidence and peace of mind that your book will come off the press looking polished and professional—ready to compete in the marketplace.

What word processing program should I use?

Stick with the big one: Microsoft Word. This program checks your spelling and grammar and offers an excellent thesaurus. It is also the standard word processor in the e-world. Using a different software program for word processing is like typing a manuscript on colored paper: There is no advantage or point to it.

Try to avoid an abbreviated version of the real thing that comes loaded for free with many computers. There is a reason why it's free.

Remember: Book manufacturers do not print from word processing files. All files must be converted to an acceptable format.

Writer: "I'm not up to writing today, sweetheart.
I fell through the front door screen."
Spouse: "Oh, you poor dear! You've strained yourself."

DESIGN QUESTIONS

What typeface should I use for my text?

If you are doing your own layout, you should use a serif typeface, or font, if you want your text to be easy to read. Serifs are the small extensions or *ticks* on the bases and tops of letters. They lead the eye from one letter to the next, making the type easier to read. The typeface for this book is Veljovik Book, an elegant serif font. Many authors use Times New Roman because it is the default font in Microsoft Word. For book printing Times New Roman is somewhat unpredictable, however, and you won't find many books in a store that use this font. Better to avoid it if you can.

If you want something different, I suggest Century Schoolbook, Baskerville, Garamond, Goudy Old Style, or another easily readable serif font. Avoid sans serif fonts—*sans* from the French, meaning *without*. This sentence is written in Arial, a sans serif typeface, and reading several pages of it will tire your eyes. Serif fonts are good for body copy, and sans serif fonts are good for headers and subheaders, which is the scheme we've used throughout this book.

What margins do you recommend?

Probably the thing that amateurs neglect most often is to allow enough space for margins. The printer requires white space all around the page, including around running heads and folios. We suggest a minimum of 0.75" of white space in the gutter (center of the book) and 0.5" on the other three sides. You should never have anything in print closer than 0.25" to the edge of your trim.

How do I prepare my text for the printer?

One of the most significant changes that has taken place since the first printing of this book is the file format most requested by book printers. PDF appears to have won the race when it comes to preferred text format. It works with virtually all imagesetters, platesetters, and digital output devices. Most popular file formats, including MS Word, WordPerfect, and MS Publisher, can be converted to PDF. Like PostScript, PDF is a *locked* format, so there usually is no problem with reflows when the files are opened on different computers. A PDF document can be read by Acrobat Reader or an equivalent. Acrobat Reader is available for free at many Web sites.

Like everything else in the electronic world, the meaning of the word *easy* is relative. It may take a little time and patience, but for all you Word users, it's certainly easier and cheaper than purchasing and learning to use InDesign or Quark. Of course, if you'd like, you can do what I did and hire the designers at *SelfPublishing.com*, who, for a reasonable fee, will lay out your book in the proper format. Because our computers save us thousands of dollars in typesetting costs, we should be able to afford several hundred dollars for the services of someone who specializes in ensuring that our books make it from PC to press smoothly and efficiently.

When is a good time to use Microsoft Word to lay out my book?

Simply put: Never! Microsoft anything does not work very well with any printing process except your desktop printer. Bill Gates started out as a computer geek, not a commercial book printer. Word is a word processing program. As such they both do a good job of processing words. Spell checker, grammar checker, thesaurus—all of these are great tools to help you write a better manuscript. However, when it's time to turn your manuscript into a book, you will be wasting a lot of time and effort by trying to make a word processing program act like a page layout program.

The primary problem is that the way Word behaves on your machine depends on your printer drivers. What looks great on your screen may look entirely different on another computer with a whole different set of printer drivers. Your carefully positioned headers can suddenly move to the next page! A Word document can be converted to a PDF document (a file format that commercial printers can use), but you usually encounter the same problem in making the conversion. A 256-page Word document can suddenly turn into a 292-page PDF document. You may struggle for dozens of hours trying to jerry-rig your document to *look* like the book layout on your screen, only to find that once you convert the file to PDF for printing, the result is a jumbled mess.

If you really have the urge to design and lay out your book, you'll need to invest in a page layout program like InDesign or Quark and learn how to use it. These are fairly expensive programs and not particularly easy for the novice to understand. I do know plenty of authors, though, who have gone this way and found the experience to be personally rewarding. If this doesn't sound exciting, however, you can do a little shopping and discover that the price to have your book professionally designed and laid out does not cost as much as buying a layout program. In my opinion, you will be much better off saving yourself the money, time, and aggravation and investing it in a marketing program for your book.

*It's that 99% of the vanity presses
that give the rest a bad name!*

What if I have only hard copy and no *electronic* file?

Back in the old days we used to call it camera copy. Few printers have *cameras* anymore so the term *camera copy* does not have any real meaning, in a literal sense, so we'll call it *hard copy*. Nowadays, hard copy usually consists of a copy of an old book where electronic files are not available. In this case the printer can scan the pages in the book and use the resulting scan for printing. Keep in mind that you can not easily make corrections to these files, so while this is fine for reprints of old out-of-print books; it is not good for new titles. If you are struggling with trying to convert your word file to PDF, don't try to short-cut the system and send a print-out to the printer to scan. I guarantee that you will want to make corrections and will end up with a mess, if you do that.

What can you tell me about *text proofs*?

Let me answer that by first going back thirty-five years or so in the printing industry. If you aren't interested in a little history lesson, you can jump right to the next question. If you are, I think you'll find this interesting. Back then, writers used manual typewriters to create their manuscripts and Linotype operators set type in hot metal. There were several different proof stages before a book got to the printer. The first stage was the galleys. Individual lines of type were keyed in and molded in metal on a Linotype machine. A line of type was as thick as the point size, as long as the specified column width, and about half an inch high. That was the *line of type*. Compositors placed these lines of type in long trays called galleys, line by line, and locked them together to keep them from falling apart. The term *leading* came from the slivers of lead put between the lines of type to space them out on the page. With an order to *increase the leading* a compositor physically added strips of lead in between the lines.

Once all the type was in place in the galleys, an ink impression of them was taken on long paper sheets, and these were called the galley proofs. They were then proofread, and corrections were made. If a line of type contained an error, the old slug of type for that line was removed and a new line was created and inserted. Corrections at this stage were fairly inexpensive; it was not uncommon to go through two or three sets of galley proofs before going to the next step.

Once the writer or editor approved the final galley proofs, a designer pasted them into page layouts. Based on those layouts, the compositor took the galleys of metal type and composed them into page trays, leaving spaces for the placement of halftones (pictures), maps, charts, pen-and-ink drawings, and so on, which were dropped in later by the printer. Once these pages were locked, the page proofs were printed from the composed pages of type. Changes at this stage of the process were much more expensive.

After the page proof was approved, a camera-ready reproduction proof, or repro proof, was made from the same metal page type. Repro proofs were printed on better paper, and special attention was given to print quality because the approved repro proofs were sent to the printer to make negatives for offset printing.

Once the printer received the camera-ready repro proof, he photographed it on a litho camera and made film negatives. These negatives were then taped, or stripped, onto large imposition sheets called film flats. Their layout corresponded to the position of the pages on the press sheet. (A 6 x 9" book with sixty-four pages was typically printed as two 32-page sections, or signatures, on a 38 x 50" sheet of paper.) At this stage, the printer made another proof by exposing the film flats on photographic paper that was developed in a chemical solution, and then hung on a clothesline to dry. When the photosensitive paper developed, the type appeared as dark blue on a white background. Thus the term *blueline* came into existence. The proof paper could only be developed on one side, so the pages were glued together, back to back, to show the actual layout of the book. A folded and trimmed book of glued-together bluelines functioned as the final proof before going to press. Printers referred to this book of bluelines as the bookblue.

Making corrections at the bookblue stage of production was quite expensive. If an editor caught a minor typographical error, the typesetter had to set a new line of type to replace the flawed one in the page tray. He then had to make another repro proof before the printer shot another negative and stripped that correction into the film flats.

Why am I telling you all this when the only Linotype machines remaining are either in museums or perhaps somewhere in the New York Times or Chicago Tribune building waiting for the last union Linotype operator to retire? The reason I've gone into such detail is that we cling to many of the terms from that bygone era, and, out of habit, we sometimes expect to see certain proofs that not only are unnecessary, but no longer exist!

Today, you, as the writer, create the equivalent of galleys as you type away at your word processor. Back in the old days, you didn't dare change the column width because it meant resetting the entire manuscript. Today, you can change the column width in a few seconds, and make any other changes you want right there on the screen in front of you. Hit your print button and you've got a galley proof that you can read on the train, or in bed, or carry around in your briefcase to show your friends. Format your type into actual pages and print them, and you've got your page proofs. You can even use your laser printer to print them front and back, just as they will appear in your book.

You're in charge now. You and your computer have replaced the old prepress process.

Should I have my book *cover/casewrap/jacket* professionally designed?

Yes. It is worth every penny. The next time you're in the bookstore, take the time to examine the cover designs. I can write with confidence that ninety-nine out of every one hundred of those book covers were professionally designed. If there are exceptions to this rule, they will be found in the bookstore section featuring local authors, and nine out of ten of those books will have covers designed by people who knew what they were doing.

Normally, you are attracted to a person because of his or her face. The cover is your book's face. Acne, bed-head, and snarled lips discourage interest in your book, if you get the analogy.

What is a *hybrid text design*?

This is the ultimate text layout for the budget minded shopper. It combines some do-it-yourself elements, along with minimal designer interaction. If you have a basic fiction or prose-style non-fiction book and some time to invest, you can't beat the price. You choose from several standard design options. Keep in mind, if your text contains photos or charts, or anything beyond straight running text, you will not qualify for this service.

What is a *hybrid cover*?

These cover designs are based on templates that you choose from a large selection. If you have your own image already selected for your cover and you have a pretty good idea of what you want, chances are there will be a template to your liking, and this option saves you money.

What is the difference between a *cover*, a *jacket*, and a *casewrap*?

These are related in that they all print and wrap around the text pages of your book. A *cover* is the term we use to describe what wraps around a paperback book. *Jackets* and *casewraps* are on hardcover books. The difference here is that a jacket is loose (i.e., it can be removed from the book) and has flaps. Casewraps are more like a cover in that they wrap the binder boards, which are what wraps your text pages. Casewraps are typically used on children's books, field guides, school textbooks, cookbooks, and short-run hardcover guides.

Secretary: "Sir, there's an invisible writer at the door."
Editor: "Tell him I can't see him now."

Do I need to use four colors to create an effective cover/jacket/casewrap?

There is no black or white answer to this question (no pun intended)! Look at your own books. Some of them, I'm sure, have very attractive two-color covers. The designer who did them really had three colors to work with since the white of the paper was already there, so they actually had a whole variety of color shades to work with. It's possible to save some money using a well-designed one- or two-color cover.

You might think that the printing cost difference between one-, two-, and four-color covers would be substantial, but the industry has changed, and four-color covers are most often only a few cents more than one- or two-color covers. While two-color covers can be nice, spend some time in a bookstore looking at different covers. If there are two travel books, one with a two-color and the other with a four-color cover, which one do you think looks more attractive? Keep in mind that there is no two-color option in digital printing; it's either black or four-color, similar to your desktop printer at home.

Remember that if you are using a bar code, it must be black or a color dark enough to be scanned. Keep this in mind when counting the number of colors on your cover. Building your bar code out of different colors is not a very good idea—you'll find very few books with anything other than black bar codes.

How do I know how wide the spine will be?

There's a simple formula that determines the spine width. Just take the number of pages in your book and divide that figure by your text paper's ppi (pages per inch). Where do you get the ppi? It depends on what kind of paper you're using, and it usually appears on the printer's estimate or quote. If for some reason it doesn't appear there, ask the printer for it, or see the spine width calculator in the Production Center at *SelfPublishing.com*.

Let's say your book has two hundred pages and you are printing it on a web press using Alternative offset, which has a ppi of 400. Then the width of your book's spine will be 200 ÷ 400, or half an inch. That's for a paperback. For a hardcover book, you have to allow for the thickness of the boards. The easiest way to do this accurately is to have your printer provide you with a layout guide. Layout guides are available at *SelfPublishing.com* in the Production Center.

How do I prepare my cover/jacket/casewrap for the printer?

Let's deal with the front, the spine, and the back of the cover in that order. On the front, put the book title, the subtitle, and the author. Place any graphics you want here. On the spine, the author's last name is usually at the top, the book title is in the center, and the publisher is identified at the bottom. On the back put a four-sentence description of your book. You can put endorsements here, too. Leave space for a very short bio on the author, a photograph of the author, and the ISBN and bar code.

These are the traditional places to put all of these things, but, of course, you can break any or all of the rules whenever you want! Remember, however, that you do want to sell your book, so people have to know very quickly why they should buy it.

If you are designing your cover, make sure you have some *bleed*. If your artwork goes all the way to the edge, it must extend at least one-eighth inch more, so when the book is trimmed there will be no white paper showing. This extra one-eighth inch is the *bleed*. If your printer is asking for more than one-eighth inch bleed, you should rethink your choice of printers. If their equipment can't mange to hold a +/- one-eighth inch tolerance, there is plenty of equipment out there that will. Remember that if you are using a bar code, it must be black or a color dark enough to be scanned. Avoid making small type a color. Cut out the cover and wrap it around a book on your shelf. How does it look now?

When you put your cover on disc, you must include all the fonts and graphics you have used. It's also a good idea to include any items that have been embedded in other programs during the design process. Then, if there's something wrong, it will be easier to fix.

If you are having a designer create the cover, explain clearly what you would like to see. You can also just give a designer an idea of what's in your book and let the expert go for it! If you have covers you really like, copy them and send them along. Remember, though, you are hiring a designer, not commissioning an artist to create an original work for you. A designer at *SelfPublishing.com* told me a story about one customer who wanted a cover showing a cave halfway up a mountain, a bear and a donkey sitting on a nearby ledge, symbols from the *I Ching* surrounding the door of the cave, and the moon setting behind the mountain! What the author needed in this case, they concluded, was not a cover designer but an illustrator. In cases like this, the illustrator and designer work together to achieve the final desired result.

A good designer will take your concept and give you something that will work. Remember, despite what you have heard, you *can* sometimes judge a book by its cover.

Editor: "I'll hire you at $300 a week and up it to $600 a week in six months."
Writer: "I think I'll just come back in six months."

MANUFACTURING QUESTIONS

What is a *page*?

Turn to page 1 in this book or any other book. Then turn the page. The back of page 1 is page 2. Then comes page 3, and the back of page 3 is page 4, and so on. Odd-numbered pages are always on the right, and even-numbered pages are always on the left. I know this seems obvious, but counting pages is one of the most misunderstood simple concepts in printing. Don't be fooled by thinking about *pages* and *leaves* or *sheets.*. If I tell you to turn to page 32, you just turn to page 32. You don't think, "Let's see ... that's really the second side of leaf 16 ..."; you just turn to page 32.

SelfPublishing.com has received its share of manuscripts with the pages numbered 1F and 1B (1Front and 1Back), 2F and 2B, and so on—instead of 1, 2, 3, 4, ... And yet has any of us ever seen a book in print with pages numbered 1F, 1B, 2F, 2B, 3F, 3B? Could it be mind-numbing x-rays emanating from the copy machines at Kinko's that are causing this confusion?

Remember that every page counts as a page whether it is blank or part of the text—numbered or not.

What is *text*?

Excellent question. In the book world, we use the word *text* to describe everything that is in the interior of the book, not just the words. So, if you have artwork or photos, that is all part of the *text*. If the artwork or photos are black and white, then your *text* is one-color (black). If your artwork or photos or anything else is in color, then your *text* is full color.

What is a *bleed*?

If you have an image that you want to print to the edge of the book, then that image *bleeds*. This is often done on book covers. For the printer to be able to trim the books so that the image is at the edge there must be some part of the image that gets trimmed off (or else you will have a white stripe of the paper showing). The amount that gets trimmed off is the *bleed*, and printers require a minimum of ⅛". So, be sure that you set up your files so that you have enough image to go beyond your trim. In other words, a 6 x 9" cover that bleeds all three sides on the front will really be a minimum of 6.125 x 9.25".

Is there a difference in appearance between a *digitally produced* book and one produced by standard *offset printing*?

Every time I listen to the Reader's Radio interview with Dan Poynter on "The New Book Model," I have to chuckle. Dan, of course, is the head guru of the small press publishing world. There aren't many small publishers who have not heard of his name or been to one of his seminars. While I agree with most of the things he says about publishing and marketing, I take exception to his opinion on the difference between *digital* and traditional *offset printing*. Dan states with authority, referring to digitally produced books, "They look just like any other book.... I challenge you to even tell the difference."

If you believe that the full-color printing in *USA Today* is equal to the color printing in *GQ* magazine (as many consumers do), you will probably not notice the difference between a book produced in a digital plant and one that was printed at an offset book manufacturer. Don't get me wrong. I am not saying that digital printing is bad. I am saying that it is different.

The modern digital color cover presses are very good. I threw away my *loupe* (magnifying glass used for checking registration and dot structure) years ago. Taking this into consideration, and the fact that my eyes aren't what they were thirty-five years ago when I got into the business, you can hardly tell the difference between a process color cover printed on a digital press and one printed on an offset press, as long as there is a film lamination on top of the printing. Without the lamination, it is pretty easy to tell the difference, but no experienced publisher would sell a book without a laminated cover. The main area that still needs improvement in the color digital process is that of solids or gradated screens. You can still sometimes see banding and other inconsistencies in these areas. Still, if I were to grade the overall cover appearance, I would give it a B+ versus an A for the offset cover (still on the honor roll).

Digital text printing has also come a long way. There are a couple of different processes in use, but the most common is DocuTech™ by Xerox®. In short, a Xerox® by any other name is still a Xerox®. For straight type, it looks fine. It's a much darker/denser black than offset because it's toner and not ink. It is almost an unnatural look after so many years of seeing ink on paper, although it certainly passes the "no loupe, no glasses" test.

The problem comes into play when you try to mix even the simplest graphics or halftones (images) into the text. There is no comparison between the appearance of graphics and halftones done on a digital press and those printed on a traditional offset press. If you plan on having graphics or photos you may want to see a sample. Ask your printer.

Now that we have talked about some of the more obvious differences between digital and offset, we'll move on to some of the more subtle differences. Have you ever unpacked a ream of copy paper, loaded it into a copier, and run off five hundred copies? Does the pile of *copies* have the same physical appearance as the pile of paper you loaded in the feeder tray? Ever try to put the five hundred *copies* back into the same package that the five hundred blank sheets of paper came from? Most digital processes utilize extreme temperatures to fuse the toner to the paper. This heat takes the moisture out of the paper, which tends to make the *copies* brittle as they slide fresh out of the copier. Natural humidity puts moisture back into the paper but not necessarily to the same degree as when it came out of the pack. If you leave the pile of *copies* out for a while, the pile will start to flatten, but it will never get back to the paper's initial condition; thus the appearance of the paper will be slightly changed. The offset presses that print single-color books do not use heat. The sheet that goes into the press is at the same moisture level as the sheet that comes out of the press. If you have seen a digital printing line in operation, you'll recall that the *book block* comes out of the copier and goes right into the binder. Now try to picture this pile of sheets (book block), with all the moisture drawn out of the sheets, being sealed on the binding edge with adhesive to apply the cover. You now have a book block picking up moisture on three sides and not the fourth. You can get a curl to the whole book that will never flatten out. This problem itself gives the overall finished book a C or C+ look, bringing the whole product down to a C+, which is still commercially acceptable but bothersome to many customers.

Another typical problem lies in the strength of the binding. In perfect binding, *signatures* (groups of pages) are gathered to make a book block. The binding edge goes through a grinding unit, which *roughs up* the edge so the adhesive will hold better when the cover is applied to the binding edge of the book. After the cover is applied and wrapped around the book, the book block gets trimmed on the outside, top, and bottom by either a three-knife trimmer or a flatbed cutter, making a finished book. A typical new perfect binding machine used by offset book manufacturers can cost over two million dollars. The perfect binders that are used in digital shops cost as little as $20,000 and rarely more than $100,000. The difference between the two types involves a lot more than markup. Most binders digital printers use produce little more than a glorified pad. Ninety-five percent of the complaints that I have run into with the digital product revolve around the binding, and 75% of them concern the pages falling out as the book is flattened out for reading.

As long as I am on the topic of pages falling out, I might as well talk about the main cause of this problem. Aside from the problems of inefficient grinding units and the cheaper binders applying adhesives, the main culprit is the grain of the paper. Paper is made primarily of pulp and water (as well as chemicals to regulate brightness and opacity). As the papermaking process begins, pulp is added to water to make a sort of pulp soup. As this solution moves through the paper-making machine, the pulp fibers line up in parallel rows. Moisture is removed until the mixture becomes paper. (Any paper people reading this, please excuse my simplistic description of this process.) The bottom line is that the direction in which these pulp fibers are aligned represents the *grain* of the paper. All paper has a *grain*. If you take a piece of 8.5 x 11" copy paper and fold it the 11" way, you get a nice, smooth fold. Fold the same sheet the 8.5" way and you get a ragged, irregular fold. The heavier the paper, the more pronounced this effect. You always want the grain of the paper to run parallel to the binding edge of the book. This allows the pages of the book to open naturally. If the grain is going against the bind, the book does not lay open naturally. The reader will tend to flatten the book to keep it from snapping shut. As the book is repeatedly flattened, the spine eventually breaks. Once this happens, the pages start falling out of the book.

Most digital presses print an 8.5 x 11" sheet of paper. Except for special orders, the grain of the paper is 11". That yields a wrong-grain 5.5 x 8.5" book. If short-grain paper is specially ordered so that the 5.5 x 8.5" product is correct, it yields a wrong-grain 8.5 x 11" book. Judging from the sample books that I've received from various digital printers, only a small minority seem concerned about using correct-grain paper.

When all is said and done, I wind up back at my original statement: Digital books aren't necessarily bad, but they are different. Your best bet in ordering digital printing is to find an old-line book printer who made the move to digital printing rather than one who has always been a digital printer. Chances are the old-line printer is used to running books with correct-grain paper and binding books that don't fall apart. Chances are also good that he is running a true perfect binder, not the bargain basement version run by most digital shops. Most straight digital book printers lack the experience to know any better or the money to do anything about it. As a buyer you need to be clear in you mind as to what you are buying. The digital book printers used by *SelfPublishing.com* were all producing good books long before anyone ever heard the term POD (print on demand). If a printer is quoting for a run under about seven hundred and fifty copies, he is probably figuring to run on a digital press. Do yourself a favor when dealing with one of these printers and confirm that at least the paper grain to be used is correct. If the printer representative doesn't know what you are talking about or tells you that it doesn't matter, hang up the phone and try someone else.

Finally, no matter how much you want it to happen, you are not going to achieve A or even A- quality with digital printing. If that is what you require, you need to either raise your quantity to run at an offset printing plant or put your money back in your pocket and try again in few years or so.

What is a *galley*?

If you read the long version of the "What kind of text proof will I receive" question, you learned what a *galley proof* was. The term *bound galleys* came from binding together those original galley proofs into a book format to be sent out to the various media for review purposes. While galleys have gone the way of the dinosaurs, the phrase *bound galleys* has still hung around. This term is used interchangeably with the term ARC or Advanced Reader Copies. While a lot of lip service is given to this subject in the various online news groups, they are a waste of time and money for the self-publisher. Let's take a quick sobriety check. If you think you are going to get reviewed in the *New York Times*, please refer to the last question in the book concerning appearing on Oprah. It's not going to happen. I suggest that everyone print an initial short digital run as a last pass prior to any long press run. In your mind you can call this an ARC or a bound galley, but it's really just a last shot for you to look at your book before you invest a lot more money in printing. If you print "Unedited Galleys for Review Purposes Only" like the big guys, the only thing you have accomplished is to make those books unsellable. A few words are not going to convince the *New York Times* into thinking you are a big publisher. Your chances for a major review are just as good (probably better) if you simply print a "Review Copy" label and stick on the front cover.

Is white considered a color in printing?

No. The white of the paper never counts as a color. A one-color cover is one ink color on white paper, so unless you fill up the whole cover with that ink—it could be black or red or green or any other color—you'll have contrast. You start with blank cover stock and you add one ink to it, and you have a one-color cover. A two-color cover is two colors on white, and a three-color cover is three colors on white. Designers often use screens to get other tints or colors without having to pay for them. For example, a 50% screen used with black will yield a gray tint in the area screened, and a 50% screen of red will yield a pink tint, and so on. In addition, the combination of two screens gives the effect of a third color (blue plus yellow equals green, yellow plus red equals orange, and so forth). Once you get to four-color, the rules change.

Sometimes people new to publishing make the mistake of not thinking of black as a color. It surely is.

What *trim size* should I use?

Trim size relates to subject matter and perceived value. There are five basic trim sizes. The mass-market paperback size is 4 x 6.875". This size is associated with both fiction and nonfiction, and it represents the low end of the retail price range. Short-run methods do not efficiently produce books of this size. You need a press run of about 10,000 + books to obtain a unit cost that works with a standard pricing formula. This size almost never works for the self-publisher. The perceived value is too low and doesn't work with the higher printing costs of short runs.

The *small publisher* answer to this size is 5 x 8". This is not really a standard *big publisher* size, but it is very *press efficient* on the short run digital printing equipment.

The standard trade paperback size can be either 5.5 x 8.5" or 6 x 9". These sizes do not work efficiently on most short-run processes. A standard DocuTech™ is limited to printing only four 5.5 x 8.5" or 6 x 9" pages at a time, versus eight pages at a time using a trim size of 5 x

8". The longer-run presses are different. If you are running at least five hundred copies, the 6 x 9" trim size costs only about 5% more than the 5.5 x 8.5" and either size is quite press efficient. Trade paperback books carry a higher retail price than mass-market books. Trade paperbacks are also sometimes called *quality paperbacks*. Generally, *quality* refers to the offset paper used.

The standard textbook size is 7 x 10". Many software manuals and many cookbooks are also printed in this size.

The workbook size is 8.5 x 11". This size is standard for both short-run and long-run equipment. *How to books* and other nonfiction works fit this trim size well. You would never consider this size for a novel, however. For short runs, there's no price difference between this size and 7 x 10".

Should I be looking outside the United States to print my black-and-white book?

Generally the answer is no. Papers, plates, and ink—the main materials in the printing process—cost the same here as they do anywhere else in the world. Printing presses and related equipment cost the same no matter where you go and must be maintained the same way worldwide. In the United States, we actually pay less than foreign consumers for uncoated book paper because the paper mills are right here.

Many foreign countries do have an advantage in labor rates, but it is a small one. Let's say that the unit cost of a book is $4, and $3 of that represents the cost of materials. That leaves only $1 that can be discounted. If the foreign labor rate is one-fourth that of the United States, there is a savings of 75 cents per book; but the books still must be shipped. In the end, the total savings amounts to pennies, if that. When you factor in the time needed for your books to reach this country by boat, foreign printing looks even less attractive. Stick with "Made in America."

Why can't I just go to a local printer?

I believe a personal anecdote will best answer this question. Several years ago I produced a monthly ad-supported comedy magazine called the *Broadneck Baloney*. It was thirty-two 8.5 x 11" pages, printed in two colors on 50# offset paper, and the circulation was ten thousand. Although I live in Maryland, I got the lowest price from a firm in Dover, Delaware, that used a huge web press to print all thirty-two pages at the same time. It took them less than two hours to strip, print, fold, and staple my publication. Of course, they were very busy, and I had to schedule my time on their press in advance if I wanted to meet my first-of-the-month publication date.

During this period, a local printer prepared my letterhead, business cards, and flyers. He also distributed about a hundred of my *Broadneck Baloney* copies to his other customers each month. He wanted to give me a price on the *Broadneck Baloney*. Without telling him the price I was getting in Dover, I said that he couldn't possibly beat it. He insisted. I said, "Okay." Several days later he sent me a written bid. It stated that he would be so kind as to print 10,000 copies of *Broadneck Baloney* for a mere $8,260. I was paying $1,240 in Dover.

Yes, I could have just gone to my local printer to have my comedy magazine manufactured on his one-color press that printed two pages at a time—if it weren't for that $7,020 I'd be throwing out the window!

What is true of magazines in this regard is true of books. One advantage of working with *SelfPublishing.com* is that their experts will make certain that the printer with the right press for your specifications prints your book.

What paper is best for the text?

Paper makes up over 50% of the cost of the average printing job. The right paper choice for your book project can mean the difference between losing money and making a profit. Paper is sold like meat—by the pound. Simply put, heavier paper costs more. Let's compare 50# ("fifty-pound") and 60#. The 60# is 20% heavier than the 50#. Assuming text paper makes up 50% of the cost of your book (that percentage increases with quantity), then using 50# paper instead of 60# will cut 20% or more off your paper cost, and 10% or more off your total cost.

Use one of the standard papers most publishers use for their books. Stay away from paper salesmen with swatch books. His or her detailed discussion of a paper's opacity, color, finish, brightness, and groundwood content is usually not intended to save you money. I suggest you select one of the stocks offered by *SelfPublishing.com*.

Would using 20# bond paper for my text save money?

Good question. The answer is no. Let me explain why. The poundage of text paper in the United States is determined by the weight of five hundred sheets measuring 25 x 38". That measurement of area is called the basis size. Five hundred sheets of 50# text paper measuring 25 x 38" weigh 50 pounds. Five hundred sheets of 60# text paper measuring 25 x 38" weigh 60 pounds, and so on.

The weight of bond paper, used mostly in copy shops, is calculated using a different basis size—17 x 22". Five hundred sheets of 20# bond measuring 17 x 22" weigh 20 pounds. Five hundred sheets of 24# bond measuring 17 x 22" weigh 24 pounds, and so on. If you do the math to compare the two different systems of weight measurement, guess what? The 20# bond is the same as the 50# offset, and the 24# bond is the same as the 60# offset. Why two different basis sizes for text and bond paper were established, I don't know, and no one can tell me. At least now it won't confuse you any more.

"I was an archaeologist before I became a self-publisher."
"Really? What made you get out of archaeology?"
"My career was in ruins."

Does a heavier text paper mean a thicker book?

Not necessarily. Because of different manufacturing techniques, the weight of the paper and the number of pages per inch (ppi) are not always proportional. The 50# white offset suggested by *SelfPublishing.com* is 512-540 ppi, and the 60# offset is 434 ppi. But if you look at the 50# natural offset, it has almost the same ppi as the 60# white. If you're thinking of printing your book on 60# offset for bulk, you could use 50# natural getting the same bulk and feel at a lower price. The 50# natural costs a little more per pound, but you don't need as many total pounds.

What about the Alternative Offset and the recycled offset? When should I use these?

SelfPublishing.com recently added two new papers and deleted one. The two new additions are 45# Alternative Offset and 50# Offset with 30% post-consumer recycled content. The 45# Alternative Offset is not quite as bright as the regular 50# offset but is a good, less expensive alternative. It is priced a little lower than the 50# offset, and is a popular sheet with the larger publishers. The one downside of this sheet is that it will start to yellow sooner than the regular 50# offset because of the groundwood content. If you don't expect to sell out your press run in a year or less, I wouldn't recommend using it.

The 50# recycled offset, on the other hand, is more expensive than the regular 50# offset because the larger publishers have been slow in increasing their demand for recycled paper, making it more expensive to produce. It looks more or less the same as the regular 50# offset. If political correctness is number one on your list, this may be the paper stock for you. You can actually sleep well at night using any of the suggested papers though. None of them are made from Rain Forest trees or the Giant Redwoods or any other ancient forests. The trees used in our papers are grown and harvested just like any other crop. Even the regular 50# is made with 15% post consumer waste, which used to be great until the people who determine what is great determined that 30% was the minimum to be able to say it is recycled. Depending on the political tide in Washington, that number could go to 100% in the future, making the 30% recycled guys the "bad guys." I suggest that you go *SelfPublishing.com* and try pricing your book in different ways. You will definitely be a trendsetter if you use the recycled paper, but you still need to make money to stay in business. Very few, if any, books command a higher retail price solely from being printed on recycled paper.

What kind of cover paper should I use for my book?

I recommend what we have used for this book—10-point cover stock, coated on one side. It is measured not by weight, but by caliper. That means if you stack up one thousand sheets of 10-point cover stock, it will be about ten inches high. What will its weight be? You can't determine that exactly, because different paper mills produce different densities of cover stock. Three stacks of one thousand sheets of 10-point cover stock from three different paper mills will most likely have three different weights.

What are the different ways I can have my book printed?

Digital Printing

Because it is relatively new, digital printing gets a lot of attention these days. Digital is associated with on-demand, which is associated with short runs, low cost, and fast turnarounds. Do most on-demand printers live up to the hype? Not really, but—it's better than it was even a few years ago and it's definitely here to stay.

Is this process fast for short runs of books? Sure it is. Is it less expensive than other forms of short-run printing? Until a few years ago, despite the hype, the answer was no. Now the answer is yes, depending on the company, equipment, and pricing philosophy. *SelfPublishing. com* used short run offset for all quantities from one hundred to five hundred up until about five or six years ago because it was less expensive than digital. That is no longer the case.

The path to the new *economies* of digital printing probably started with the entrance of competition on the equipment side of the equation. Where Xerox once enjoyed a near monopoly, there are now many newcomers to the field of digital printing. Increased competition on the equipment side has had a general lowering effect on the price of all digital book printing.

What are the strengths of digital printing? A digital press can take the digital files from your computer and go right to print. In the case of text type, it's hard to tell the difference between the different types of equipment.

What is the major weakness of digital printing? There is no real quantity discount. Your unit cost stays more or less the same no matter what quantity you print. That's great if you want a small number of copies, but not so great if you want several thousand copies. Digital printing is generally more expensive than offset in quantities over five hundred.

Short-Run Offset

Short-run offset printing is a scaled-down version of the traditional book manufacturing process. The average short-run press prints eight pages of a 5.5 x 8.5" book at a time, compared with thirty-two, sixty-four, or one hundred twenty-eight pages at a time for the traditional sheetfed book press. While the traditional sheetfed press uses metal plates, the short-run press uses less expensive plates made directly from your digital files. This process has all but been replaced entirely with digital printing.

Traditional Sheetfed Printing

The traditional sheetfed press sees little use in today's book manufacturing. I can almost guarantee that if your book is being printed on a sheetfed offset press, you are paying more than you need to. This method used to fill the gap between short-run sheetfed and web presses. That is no longer true because of the fact that the newer web presses are efficient right down to around five hundred copies, where the short-run digital presses leave off. There is still room for traditional sheetfed printing, however. Few web presses and hardly any digital presses can print on coated paper. A sheetfed press using metal plates on coated paper does a much better job on halftones than any other process. Using a standard paper and trim size, the traditional sheetfed press cannot compete with modern web presses. If you want coated glossy paper for a lot of halftones, and/or your book has an odd trim size, traditional sheetfed printing may be the best choice for you.

Web Offset

A web press prints using rolls of paper, which are cheaper than sheets; and at the end of the press run, it delivers a folded signature instead of a flat sheet, thus consolidating two book manufacturing processes. Running speeds sometimes exceed twenty-five thousand impressions per hour. This compares with about two thousand per hour on the short-run presses, and about five thousand per hour on the larger sheetfed presses.

The amount of makeready spoilage used to be very high on web presses, making them economical only for quantities over five thousand or so. This has all changed for those printers who have replaced their decades-old webs with the more efficient up-to-date machinery. Modern-day makereadies are extremely efficient and spoilage is low. The advantages of a web press are speed and cost. If you are printing more than five hundred copies of a standard-size book on uncoated paper, there are no disadvantages to printing on the web.

"How did you get into self-publishing?"
"I decided to go into it after I lost my job because of something my boss said."
"What did he say?"
"You're fired."

What is a POD Printer?

Under the strict definition of the term, there are very few true POD printers (one book at a time). Under the evolved definition (short run) there are many. Whatever the case, the printer is the one who actually owns the equipment that prints and binds the books.

How many books should I print?

Not counting books used for promotion, you shouldn't print a single book more than you can sell.

If your book size is 5 x 8", 5.5 x 8.5", 6 x 9", 7 x 10" or 8.5 x 11", you can get instant prices at *SelfPublishing.com*. Quantities for these sizes start as low as a hundred. You know what your budget is. Get prices on one hundred, five hundred, one thousand, or other appropriate amounts and think it through. The larger the quantity, the lower the unit cost. But what good is the lowest unit cost if most of the books stay stacked up in the garage?

When you are analyzing your unit cost, keep in mind that you will have to offer large distributors like *Amazon.com* a 60% discount off the retail price in order for them to sell your book.

What is four-color process?

The term *four-color* refers to the three process colors of yellow, cyan (blue), and magenta (red) plus black. From these four colors, printed in screens of dots, one on top of the other, you can make almost all the colors in the spectrum. Any time you see a *full-color* photograph printed in a book or magazine, it's four-color process. Any time a cover looks like it has more than two colors, it's probably a four-color cover. The next time you notice a blurry picture in a color newspaper, take a closer look and you'll see how the process works. The picture is blurry because the press was *out of register*. Sometimes the register is so bad you can actually see the different-color dots.

Can I print color pictures in my one color trade book cost-effectively?

No. Although prepress costs have fallen dramatically in the last decade or so, four-color process printing is still expensive. Printing a full-color sixteen-page signature in a 5.5 x 8.5" book will cost you about $800 computer-to-plate prep and proofs, and another $1,000 or so for the plates and printing. If you're printing only five hundred books, that's a unit cost of just under $4 per book just for the sixteen-page color signature. Using a standard markup of five or six times the production cost to figure your retail price, you would have to add an additional $24 per book to make the numbers work out profitably.

I have discussed my *Secrets of the Parthenon* series of books—all four-color throughout—with the experts at *SelfPublishing.com*. They estimate that I will have to print twenty-thousand copies of each book in order to get my unit cost low enough to set a retail price under $20. These are very specialized books that wouldn't make sense to print in black and white. I need some investors.

So, unless you have a special case as I do, using color in the body of your book is not a good idea. The exception to this is children's picture books.

What kind of text proof will I receive for my one-color book?

The final proofs that printers offer today vary depending on the printing method. *SelfPublishing.com* makes sure each customer gets a final proof that is compatible with the printing technology used for his or her book. These final printer proofs are your last chance to catch mistakes before you go to press. Funny things can happen between your initial type input and the time when your book reaches the printing press. The obvious thing to check at this stage is that all the pages are there and are all in the right order. Some of the not-so-obvious things to check are to make sure that no formatting changes occurred when you converted to PDF from your application program. Punctuation sometimes changes, and fonts also sometimes change. It's up to you to catch these problems in the proof. Once you have approved the proof, you have bought the books that match that proof. We had a case in one of the printings of this book where we gave the identical PDF file to five printers to print the five signatures on five different presses. When printed, four of the five were perfect. The fifth was missing all the punctuation marks. In the end, we had to pay for the incorrect pages because we had seen the proof. The fact that four other printers took the exact same file and printed it perfectly meant nothing. Don't let this happen to you. Check your proof.

What kind of *cover proof* will I receive?

Your designer's computer is capable of doing things that only a decade or so ago were reserved for prepress film houses with millions of dollars worth of equipment. Today, in most cases, when your designer finishes your cover, it's ready for press.

If you are running a one- or two-color cover, your designer's laser proof should be enough. The printer will print the PMS (Pantone Matching System) colors that you specify on your order.

With a four-color cover, things are a little different. You should not rely on your designer's laser proof unless you have a fairly wide window of tolerance between your proof and the printed cover. You should also never count on what you see on your computer screen to be more than a general representation of what will be printed on the final product. But what can you rely on?

Your best color proof is a press proof, but domestic printers rarely supply these because of their prohibitive cost. The next best proof used to be a film proof like a chromalin or matchprint, but the printers' move away from film towards direct-to-plate has made film proofs a thing of the past. That leaves us with a digital proof. Over the past several years, digital proofs have gained widespread acceptance. They are not as good as press proofs or film proofs, but that's progress. Remember that no one but you has seen your original cover. The money you save using today's technology far outweighs any minor color variation in the final product.

What is perfect binding, and should I use it for my book?

Perfect binding is also called adhesive binding or paperback binding. There are also some patented processes such as Lay-Flat™ and Ota-Bind™. These processes gather pages together in a stack, grind off one-eighth of an inch of the backbone, rough it up, and apply adhesive. Then the machinery applies the paper cover to the glued book block, squares it off, and trims the three other sides to make the final book.

Perfect binding is the least expensive form of bookbinding, and most self-publishers use it. The perfect binding process is efficient down to as few as one hundred copies. Perfect binding creates a flat spine where the title, author, and publisher are printed. Stores like this because they can display the book spine out, saving them valuable shelf space. The downside is that libraries generally prefer to buy hardcover books.

What about saddle stitching?

Saddle stitching is an inexpensive binding method for books of sixty-four pages or less. Instead of piling the signatures on top of each other, as with perfect binding, signatures are wrapped around each other on a *saddle*, wire-stitched, and then trimmed on three sides. This binding is great if you're producing a newsletter for the local PTA—but not if you're trying to sell a book. Saddle stitching has a much lower perceived value. Because they do not have a spine, and thus would have to be displayed face out, bookstores do not want saddle-stitched books. The exceptions to this rule are certain types of children's picture books.

*Novelist: "I think I'll have my villain die after drinking
a bucket of varnish."
Editor: "That's not such a bad finish."*

What about plastic coil and spiral binding?

The mechanical binding category includes any type of coil type binding. Some printers use spiral, which is a continuous strand of wire or plastic. Some use wire-o, which works more like the old GBC plastic comb binding other than that the material is wire and not plastic. This type of binding works with cookbooks and manuals that are designed to lay completely flat. Bookstores do not like mechanical binding because there is no printed backbone so they can't be put on the shelf spine out. There are variations of the basic mechanical binding, such as concealed and semi-concealed, but these are not bindings that the self-publisher should be thinking of spending money on. You will never earn it back on the other end.

How about hardcover binding?

Hardcover or case binding is certainly the top-of-the-line type of binding. It is accepted by all retail outlets and libraries and has a much higher perceived value. It is also the most expensive style of binding, especially in low quantities, so it presents a financial roadblock to most self-publishers. Within the hardcover category there are many options, such as: sewing versus adhesive; cloth versus paper; stamping; and a casewrap and/or a printed jacket. In the spirit of "tires off the rack," *SelfPublishing.com* has come up with a standard that gives the self-publisher an affordable option, although I rarely suggest a hardcover first edition other than under special circumstances. Simon & Schuster can do a large hardcover roll-out followed by a trade paperback version followed by a mass market paperback. Most self-publishers are much better off buying more trade paperbacks then far fewer hardcover copies for the same total dollars.

> *Writing teacher: "Can you name two pronouns?"*
> *Inattentive student: "Who, me?"*

What are *endleaves*?

End leaves (also called *endpapers* or *ends*) are actually four pages each. In the endleaf at the front of the book, page "one" is glued down, pages "two and three" face you when you open the book and page "four" is the back of page "three." (The endleaf at the back of the book has page four glued down.) End leaves are necessary to hold your printed pages into the hardcover binding. Typically they are different paper than the rest of the book. In the *SelfPublishing.com's* programs, the one color trade books have plain (white) ends and the full-color children's books are printed in a single color (most people pick a PMS color). Note that these pages are *not counted* into the total page count. Not all hard cover books have end leaves. A book without ends is called *self-ended*. In a *self-ended* book, the eight pages of end leaves are counted into the page count. For example, a thirty-two page self-ended book has thirty-two pages out of which eight pages are end leaves and twenty-four pages are the story. In a self-ended book, there is a visible difference in the way the book looks as you open it, too. As you shop around for printing prices it is important that you watch out for whether you are being quoted a *plus* end leaves or *self-ended* product.

Why don't cannibals eat self-publishers? Because they know that you can't keep a good person down.

What about all those *terms and conditions*?

Terms and conditions are important. They lay out the basic ground rules governing the printing industry. Printing customs are the commonsense guidelines within which the printing industry works. If you believe in treating others the way you would like to be treated yourself, then you'll be fine, and the subject of printing customs won't even come up. Generally, printers are quite fair and will try to do everything within their power to make you, the customer, happy. If you act unfairly or make unrealistic demands, that's when printers are forced to stick strictly to the terms and conditions.

Let me give you a personal experience that may bring the point home. The third issue of my magazine *Broadneck Hundred* looked great. The editorial content, the photographs, and the cover were better than anything that I, or the competition, had produced. It cost a lot of money to reach that level of excellence, and I didn't have enough money left to pay the printer. Because I had produced such a "remarkable" publication, I expected the printer to release the magazines to me and let me pay for them as I sold them. Of course, the printer refused. At eight o'clock the next morning I and some associates tried to carry as many boxes of magazines out the back door of the printing plant as we could. The police stopped us. Oops! Those were not my magazines, and they wouldn't be mine until I paid for them. We were stealing.

I came to my senses, apologized to the printer, and borrowed the money to pay him. I have to chalk that one up to egotism and immaturity. I had confused the printer with the bank, and imagined that my upstart pretensions entitled me to special privileges. I had violated printing customs, but you wouldn't have had to read them to know that I was in the wrong.

I think it's basically this simple: If the printer produces commercially acceptable books that you ordered, you must pay for them.

You have an opportunity to read the Printing Trade Customs in the Production Center of *SelfPublishing.com*.

Do I have to pay for the extra books if there is an overrun?

Yes, you do have to pay for overruns up to 10% of your ordered quantity. If, for example, you order two thousand books, and twenty-one hundred or twenty-two hundred books are shipped, you must pay for the extra one hundred or two hundred books. The reason is that printers cannot estimate spoilage in the printing process exactly. According to custom, a 10% overrun or a 10% underrun counts as a complete job. You get charged for an overrun and credited for an underrun. (In other words, if you order two thousand books and receive eighteen hundred books, your order is considered complete.) If you absolutely must have a minimum quantity, then the spoilage factor doubles to 20% on the plus side. If your minimum is two thousand books, for example, then you must accept an overrun of up to twenty-four hundred. *SelfPublishing.com* does its best to hold its printers to 5% variability, and generally, orders done digitally yield the exact number ordered.

Can I get a discount on the printing bill if my books arrive late?

No—unless you have a written guarantee of a specific date, spelling out the conditions and/or consequences if that date is not met. Book printers have a general idea how long it takes to print a book in their plant. The actual time it takes depends more often on you. How well is your book prepared? How long will you hold the proofs? How many changes will you make?

SelfPublishing.com strives for realistic and consistent delivery dates. The roots of its parent company, Self Publishing, Inc., are in commercial printing, where the schedules are very tight, being geared toward trade shows and other dated events; thus they have an excellent track record for meeting deadlines. To be on the safe side, however, don't plan your publication party or schedule a book signing until you have the books in hand. You'll live longer that way.

Can I make corrections to my proofs?

Yes, you can make corrections to your proofs. Keep in mind that if they are editorial changes (author's alterations), there will be fees involved. If the errors you find involve formatting issues, the question of responsibility becomes a bit grayer. What is definitely not "gray" is that once you approve a proof, and if the printed book matches the proof, you own those copies. So check your proofs carefully, because—trust me—I have seen a lot of funky things happen at the proof stage.

The printer damaged my disc; what can I do?

If you didn't keep a copy, not much—cry maybe. It is very important that you keep copies of anything you send to the printer. This includes all text files and digital images. There are true horror stories about writers who spent years on their manuscripts, and then, not having a copy, lost them somehow. Don't take a chance; cover yourself every step of the way with copies of your work.

What about shipping costs?

Unless otherwise stated, you pay the shipping costs from the printer to the destination you specify. On smaller runs this is generally done by UPS or FedEx Ground. Shipping costs are a little like author's alterations in that nobody is happy with the costs, nobody makes any money on it, and it can be a source of contention if the cost comes as a surprise at the end. As you're pacing around waiting for your books after you've approved the proofs, do yourself a favor and research the best way to ship your books. Remember, printers are printers. They might have shipping departments but they are not in the shipping business. The printer can suggest the best way to ship your books but the money for it is coming out of your pocket. The money you save on shipping costs translates into a few less books you have to sell to break even.

What costs are not included in the estimate?

The costs to send and return your proofs to you and the printer (typically an overnight courier charge) and the actual freight charges to ship the books to their final destination are not on your original quotation or purchase order. Also, the final count can vary by 10%, so you may be charged for "extras" or credited should the count be "under."

When my book sells out, does a reprint cost less than the first printing?

No, and the reason is that because direct-to-plate technology is used with your PDF files, the same steps are done all over again. You may be able to skip a proof review, though, and that could save you a bit of time, but there are no monetary savings for reprinting.

Writer: "Last night I dreamt I was a vice."
Editor: "For God's sake, get a grip on yourself."

CHILDREN'S PICTURE BOOK QUESTIONS

This next section is new to this version of the Publishing Basics book. While there are many similarities between publishing a black & white trade book and an illustrated children's book, there are many differences. Previously, we published a special book just for illustrated children's books, but we decided to do things a little differently, this time around.

How is a title page different in a children's book?

The title page is still where you list your title, author, publisher, the city of the publisher, and usually your first picture. Children's books are different from other books in that the role of the illustrator may be more important than that of the author. You'll want to keep this in mind as you design this page.

How do I prepare my text for a children's book?

Text and art are two different things. Text typically prints in black (and black only, not black made up of four-colors). And art typically prints in four-color. So, when creating your artwork, remember to leave space where your text is going to be placed. This can be either an area with no artwork or an area that is light in color, and an area that is not too busy. Remember, you want to be able to read your type, and that won't be possible if type is in with your artwork. All files submitted to *SelfPublishing.com* need to be hi-res single page PDF files. They need a file for your text, a file for your casewrap and a file for your book jacket (if you have opted to have one).

Should I opt to have a jacket on my children's book or is a casewrap enough?

All of the books in the *SelfPublishing.com's* children's book program will have a printed casewrap. Casewraps are what *wrap* the boards used in the hardcover binding, and they go underneath the endpapers. Typically, a jacket is visually the same as the casewrap, but it is loose (i.e. it can be removed from the book, just the way we can take off a jacket). The advantage of having a jacket is that it allows you to have flaps, which are the parts that turn in at the front and the back of the book. Flaps are used to tell a bit about the book (front flap) and the author and illustrator (back flap). In other words the flaps are real estate that you use to sell your book. Many readers feel that the perceived value of a book is greater if there is a jacket. On the other hand, many parents tell me that their children just rip the jackets anyway, so they remove them as soon as they buy a book. The bottom line is that the jackets do add a bit to the cost, but the choice is yours.

I have a children's book with only eighteen pages. What should I do?

The minimum number of pages required to do a hard cover book is thirty-two (and that can include the endpapers giving you a "self-ended" book), so you will have to *add* a few pages. Usually that's easy to do with tricks such as having a *half-title page*, and a *full title page* spread (two pages) and you can often *open up* some other pages to give you what you need. Remember, many children's books have text on one page and a picture facing it, so not every page is *full*.

What types of originals are used for illustrations?

The answer to this question has changed in the last few years, because of advances in technology. Illustrations can be: original artwork; photographs; transparencies (35mm and larger); computer generated graphics (in Illustrator, Photoshop, etc.); digital photos (photos taken with a digital camera); or photo CDs (traditional film scanned to CD at time of processing). Certainly the current trend is for more and more of the artwork to be computer generated. If you do have physical artwork, keep in mind that it must be able to lie flat and the largest size that can be efficiently handled is 11 x 17". Art any larger than that needs to have a *picture* taken of it so that it can be scanned. This used to mean that a transparency was made, but now as digital cameras have improved, that is another option. If it is a transparency, that is then scanned. The last option is for the oversize artwork to be scanned on the more expensive drum scanner. Note that from a quality standpoint, when making a transparency, you are a generation away from your original. The cost can run several hundred dollars per transparency which could ruin the budget on a thirty-two-page book. So, sometimes, large artwork costs you more.

Is there one medium for illustrations that's better than another?

No, not really, but keep in mind that scanners "see" everything. So if you have layers of watercolor, or if you erased anything, those things will get picked up. If you are in doubt about how your artwork will scan, *SelfPublishing.com* suggests you send them an image to test.

My illustrations are computer generated, is that okay?

Yes, computer generated artwork is very good as long as the resolution of the images is okay. This is the way more and more artwork is produced today and is highly recommended to the self- publisher.

What size should my original art be?

Always keep in mind the trim size of your book and work proportionally with that size. In other words, if your book is going to be an 8x 8" (square) book, the artwork should be square. If it isn't, when you reduce or enlarge your artwork, something will be lost in order to have what you use be square. Also, *always allow for bleed* if you indeed want the illustrations to bleed. *Bleed* is when your color goes to the edge of the book. In order to do that, the printer needs a minimum of one-eighth inch "extra art" at each edge. So, don't have a character's head at the edge of your artwork unless you intend to crop the head on the page.

What is a *scan*?

Simply put, a scan takes a continuous tone picture and separates it into dots that a press can print from. These dots are not always visible to the naked eye. All scanners are capable of producing adequate scans for use on the Internet. Not many scanners used by the average consumer are capable of producing a scan that can be used for quality printing.

Should I provide my own scans?

Yes, if you are confident that your scanner is a good quality scanner (can scan 1200 x 1200 dpi or higher), and that whoever scanned your artwork knows a bit about what they are doing. If that is not the case, then we recommend you let *SelfPublishing.com* do the scans for you.

How do I select an endpaper color for my children's book? Or, what is a PMS color? How will my proof of the PMS color look?

The *SelfPublishing.com's* full-color children's book program is based on one side of the endpapers printing in one color. So you need to choose a color. Many book designers will have a *Pantone Book*. This is a book filled with chips of colors, and printers typically purchase inks to match these Pantone colors. We ask you to give us a *PMS color* for your endpapers. If you do not have a Pantone book, give us a swatch (in color) that you want us to match, or tell us to match a particular color in your file (the little girl's dress on page 3 for example). We will select a PMS color for you. Because our proofing system is digital, and your endpapers will print in a color that is not process (remember that we will use one ink color), the proof will be created out of four color process. This means that your endpaper proof will not be an exact match to what the finished endpaper will be once printed. No big deal, but we want you to understand what you are looking at when you see your proof.

I know that paperback binding is less expensive. Why shouldn't I use it for my children's picture book?

No matter how good your book is, you cannot sell your book for a price much higher than the current *market price*. The stores/consumers couldn't care less what you paid to print the book. They only care what the retail price of the book is as compared to other books in the category. Large publishers sell a thirty-two-page paperback color children's book for as low as $1.29, and never higher than $3 or $4. To retail books for that price, the publisher needs to be able to buy them from the printer for between twenty-five cents and seventy-five cents each. How do they do that? They print fifty thousand to one hundred thousand copies at a time, and usually group four to six different titles at a time for a total of two hundred thousand to six hundred thousand books. The truth is, you are not going to print in these quantities, so you are not going to get these printing prices, meaning that you are not going to be able to sell at the same retail price. In short—you can't compete. Hardcover books are different. Even the large publishers print much lower quantities of hardcover books. The result is that their printing costs are higher and their retail costs are higher. Add to this that the large publishers have much higher fixed costs, and the result is that you, as a small press publisher, can compete with the large publishers by only buying one thousand copies and up.

Should I use gloss or matte paper stock for my children's book?

This is up to you, one is not better than the other. Each is a coated sheet, the gloss just has more shine to it (and it is a little bit thinner than the same weight is in matte). The majority of our children's books are done on matte, but the choice is yours.

What kind of proofs will I see for full-color children's book?

The proofs you see will be digital proofs. You will receive two kinds of proofs, one is color and one is black and white. The color proofs will either be on a large sheet of paper or a trimmed version, and this proof is to check just that—your color. The paper that is used for these color proofs is not the paper your job will be printed on, so keep that in mind. The proofing paper is glossy, and is a brighter white than either of the papers we use to print from (gloss or matte). And because this proofing system is what is called a *line proof*, you may notice lines in the proof. These lines are simply a function of the proofing process and will not be visible when the job is actually printed on the printing press. (The printing press uses dots of color and ink as opposed to toner and lines as in the proof.) The black and white proof will be page size and these proofs should be used to check that all elements are on the pages where they should be. The color proofs are the proofs that will be followed at the printing press. If the proof has a red cast, the final printed product will have a red cast. No proof, however, can represent with 100% accuracy the appearance of the colors you will see in the finished product. The digital proof is about 90 % of what you'll see on the printed product. (Note: In my experience the proofs tend to be a bit richer/darker than what the printing press gives.) Without getting too technical, let it suffice to say that exact match proofs are only provided to publishers who have exact match budgets.

As a successful self-publisher, always try to be modest.
And be damn proud of it!

What does *pleasing color* mean?

Pleasing color in simple terms means that without having seen an original, the reproduction of that image is believable and pleasing. In other words, grass is green, skies are blue, skin tones are believable, etc. Almost 99% of children's book art falls into this definition. Remember, you and your friends or family are the only ones that have actually seen the original. A good test to see if your scans are okay (if you are doing them) is to show the proofs to someone who hasn't seen the original artwork... If they like the look, you are fine. Keep this in mind when you see your proofs too.

Are you saying that the printer will not match my artwork exactly?

Yes. Always keep in mind that, only you, your designer and possibly your brother, sister, mother or grandmother have actually seen your original artwork. It's sort of like the "tree falling in the woods" thing. If your color is not exact, will anybody know? The printer will print a reasonable match. If you cannot live with 90%, *stop now*! Read no further. Unless you are independently wealthy and do not mind spending a sizable portion of that wealth on book printing, you should not attempt to self-publish. Save your money. You are only going to drive yourself crazy. And even worse than driving yourself crazy (which is your right), you will drive the poor printer crazy, too. Life is too short. Pick something else to do with your money.

Domestic Printing vs. Overseas Printing: Is there a Difference?

The answer to this question is different than it was just a few years ago. Technology has changed in that short time, and that is why we are printing full color books in the USA! Today, if you have a PDF file, there no longer is a reason to go overseas to print your full-color children's book. If you do not have a PDF file, *SelfPublishing.com* can assist you with their design service. They will layout your book for an incredibly reasonable price. Being able to print full-color books in the USA is something we are very excited about. Now publishers can print as few as one thousand copies of a hardcover children's book right here in the USA, and books can be ready much faster. There are no custom's fees and no hassle of getting books delivered from a port. The books we manufacture are all the same specifications we had before, too.

I want my book to be full color, but it is not a children's book- is that okay?

Yes, that is fine. Your book can be about any subject, and that is why our pricing goes up beyond what is a typical page count for a children's book. The truth is, the printing press doesn't care what it is printing as long as it is full-color!

What can I expect in terms of timing for my children's book?

Your books will be ready to ship from the plant about five weeks from the time your disk is sent to the printer. Keep in mind that timing is based on your returning the proofs in a timely manner (typically you send them back the day or day after you receive them). It is also based on the disk having no problems. If you are using the design services of *SelfPublishing.com*, the time spent getting your files ready for the printer does not count as part of the five weeks. This schedule is a great deal shorter than what we used to offer when we had to manufacture these books overseas, and is something to consider if your other quotations are from printers in Hong Kong or elsewhere.

Self Publishing, Inc., offers single color books in quantities as low as one hundred copies. Why can't I print fewer than one thousand copies of my full-color book?

Well, actually you can print as few as twenty-five full color books. The primary reason for doing that would be to use them as samples, because production costs are still quite high. Short run digital technology for black and white printing has been around for quite some time now. The original DocuTech™ technology was designed for one purpose: to produce short run black and white books economically. On the other hand, while there have been digital color presses on the market for some time now, their original intent was more of a commercial nature like ad sheets, postcards, etc. and not book printing. Thus the *per impression* cost is okay for single sheet items, but it is very cost restrictive for multi-page items such as books. Digital presses are now in widespread use for printing book covers, but a cover is a single sheet item. All production runs of books in the *SelfPublishing.com* children's book program are printed on traditional sheetfed printing presses, which is the reason for the one thousand book minimum.

WEB SITE QUESTIONS

Web Site Development

This is a new expanded section due to the importance of the Internet as it relates to self-publishers. Back when Self Publishing, Inc., was founded, the Internet was "young and wild." The idea of doing business on the Internet was still more of a dream than a reality. Even when the first edition of the Publishing Basics book was published in 2000, dial-up modems and AOL accounts were pretty standard. It was hard enough to get text and a few graphics to load fast enough to hold people's attention, much less to actually do any business. Boy has that changed. A professional looking Web site is a key to any successful publishing venture. As with everything else in the publishing process, there is no magic involved. As important as this part of the process is, you want to watch what you spend and keep in mind, "if its too good to be true, it probably is."

The Internet is what puts the independent self-publisher on an even footing with the big guys. It's an inexpensive way to put your book in front of millions of potential customers. Have you noticed a single movie nowadays that does not have a Web site with the same name? There's a good reason. Advertising is expensive; a Web site is not. The idea is to use small, well-placed ads to attract traffic to your Web site, and then do the rest of the selling from there. You can go into as much detail about your book as you want, and that includes allowing an interested party to download a sample chapter. On your Web site, customers can order directly from you; this is your most profitable scenario. You should also promote your retail outlets by listing them with their phone numbers. Domain name registration is cheap and easy. Go to any search engine and enter the words "domain registration." You will get dozens of listings of organizations to register your name. They all have free name-search functions at their sites so you can take your time and keep entering names until you get the one you want. The final decision on the title of the Publishing Basics book was based on our being able to obtain the name *PublishingBasics.com* for our Web site. The same kind of consideration may influence the choice of your book title.

Once you have secured your name, you may need help building the actual site, and *SelfPublishing.com* has many options to choose from. Remember, you don't need to spend a lot of money to develop a decent Web presence, but like anything else worthwhile, it requires concentration and hard work on your part.

Do I need to use a Web site design company that is local to me?

Not at all. Everything can be done via email or telephone. We design Web sites for companies worldwide and rarely meet our clients in person. Our door is always open to anyone who would like to speak to us face to face, but we rarely visit anyone unless they live in our vicinity. This helps to keep our Web site design prices low!

How much do I need to spend for Web site design services?

It all depends on what you would like. A simple html Web page will cost a lot less than a dynamic page, which is usually written in PHP or ASP. Web sites can range anywhere from a couple hundred dollars to several thousands. Your best bet is to spend some time looking at other publishers' Web sites. What parts do you like? What parts do you not like? All of these things have dollar amounts attached to them for development and maintenance. It is almost always best to start small. A simple three to five page Web site is a great start. Try to put yourself in your visitors place. What do you think they want to know about you and your book and company? Whatever it is—that's what you need to let them know. Your Web site is you.

Picture yourself at a big book show with a large display to show off your book. Now picture someone coming up to your display and asking about your book. What would you say? What would you do to convince this person that he should buy your book?

This is how your Web site works, except you aren't physically there to make your "pitch." Your Web site needs to present your case for you. It's as simple as that. The only problem is that creating it isn't simple or easy. You need to plan on spending as much personal time and effort on writing and planning your Web site to sell your book, as you did to originally produce the book. But trust me, it pays off. As far as costs, you can always visit the Web site section of *SelfPublishing.com*.

What about Web Site Marketing?

Now that you have a Web site with its own URL, it's time to get the word out to the masses. For around $100 you can have the people at *SelfPublishing.com*, or someone else, list your site with several thousand search engines. There is no magic involved. It's just a software program. It's pretty good. You'll get hundreds of emails from the various sites that will have you feeling good about your site in no time. You will certainly get your money's worth. There are a handful of *must* search engines to which your site needs to be submitted by hand. That shouldn't cost you more than another $25.

One of the most effective ways to have your book pop up to the top of the search engine listings is to sign up for one of the various "pay per click" engines. Simply put, you bid against other Web sites to have your site top-listed for various keywords. The easy terms are too expensive to make sense. For example, enter the word "self-publishing" at Yahoo. The top four sites are paying over $7 per click for every visitor who clicks on their listing. Want to have some fun? Go to Google and enter the search term "self-publishing" and visit the top five "sponsored" listings. Guess what types of services are willing to pay that much to get you to visit them? Be creative. You do not need to spend more than 15 to 20 cents per click for quality traffic. The good thing with these pay engines is that you can set your own limit and you pay only if the person actually visits your site.

Do I need to pay more for a successful Web site?

Not really. The success of a Web site, generally has nothing to do with the amount of money you spend. It's all about content and giving your prospective customers enough reason to buy from you.

Do you guarantee placement in Google or other search engines?

No. Nobody can guarantee any type of ranking in Google or any other search engine. Search engine placement remains a bit of a mystery, although there is an entire industry of search engine optimization (SEO).

Back in the young and wild days of the Internet, all you needed to do is repeat the word you wanted to be "top listed" a hundred times at the bottom of your web page and your Web site would be listed #1. Those days are long gone.

SelfPublishing.com doesn't claim to be search engine optimizers but if you search self-publishing in Google, you'll usually find them in the first couple listings. How did they do this? First you have to understand that the true goal of any search engine is to match the best Web site to the search term. Ideally this search would be done by humans but that would be virtually impossible, so the decision has to be done programmatically.

The idea of SEO is to try to figure out the formula so they can optimize sites to fit the program. For lack of a better word, these SEO organizations rely on "tricks and gimmicks" to improve placement. This is a constant battle between the search engines and the SEO organizations. As soon as one gimmick implemented, the search engines figure it out and the gimmick no longer works. Rather then relying on tricks and gimmicks, I found it was easier to simply build what the search engine was looking for—the absolute best Web site to fit the search term. It's not necessarily the easiest thing to do but it is certainly the longest lasting.

At the bookstore, I asked the salesperson,
"Where's the self-help section?"
She said, "If I told you it would defeat the purpose."

What do you think of Facebook as a marketing tool for self-published books?

Not long ago I would have told you that Facebook is a useless Web site where fifteen year-olds trash talk each other and otherwise waste time. As a mater of fact, I originally opened my Facebook account to try to rummage around and see what my sixteen-year-old was up to. Today I am convinced that Facebook should be considered a primary marketing tool by every self-publisher.

I first visited Facebook to see if my sixteen-year-old had changed the "Animal House" looking picture of himself that I had heard was posted to his account. He hadn't. To the first time visitor, the Web site is just what the name implies—a virtual book of faces. The first time you go to the site you reach a very plain looking page with a green button that says "sign up." For those who don't want to sign up right away there is a search field you can use to enter a person's name. For instance, if you enter "Pramschufer," you'll come up with my picture, right on top. There are a few links about the picture like "send message" or "view friends" or "Poke him/her" but all links take you to the sign-up page. This is as far as you go without signing up. The sign-up is no big deal—go ahead and do it. Enter an email address, choose a password, enter a birthday, and you're in—or at least part way in. Now, to those same people that you did the sample search for, you can click and "Send Message" or "Poke" or "View Friends" or "Add to Friends."

As a parent, using the site for the first time, I thought I had hit pay-dirt when I hit "View Friends" because I could now see my kid's "friends"—but that was all I could see—postage sized images of all his "friends." Other than a few, "I haven't seen him/her since second grade"; this is as far as you get in the super snooper department at Facebook.

The next level of activity is adding friends, which is what Facebook is all about. It took me a while to figure out what it was all about. To add a friend, you click on the "Add to Friends" link next to the picture. The trick is that the person on the other side needs to click "Okay" before you are officially a friend. A friend basically means that you have gone from access of the person's headshot, to access to the person's home page. What is on a person's home page? Whatever they put there. I think I originally just listed my name, company name, and maybe a picture.

Finding friends is a bit tricky in the beginning. For instance, did I ask my sixteen-year-old old son to be my friend? Of course not. There was no way he was going to click okay and let me in. He doesn't even let his older brother into his "inner sanctum." I tried my oldest son first. He accepted me as a friend. That was pretty neat. I got to see some of his friends. Many of which I already knew. I clicked on a few of them and they were added to my friend list. I still didn't see any real point to the site until I did a search for publishers, or self-publishers, I forget which. Lo and behold up pops the picture of probably the best book hustling self-publisher on the planet—Relentless Aaron. I click the "Add to Friends" link and a half hour later Relentless was on my friend list. It was exploring his site that the full impact of this site became apparent.

If you are going to sell books, or anything else for that matter, you need to look your prospect in the eye, reach out and shake their hand and demonstrate how your product meets their need. Facebook gives you that opportunity. I don't see it as a "quick hit" but a place to establish a strong foundation on which to build. The site is very easy to work with and everything can be customized to meet your personal tastes. There is a great mixture of work utilities as well as playthings and other gimmicks to keep you coming back for more. If you let them, your "friends" will get to know you. As they get to know you, they get to know your product. If you are an author/self-publisher, you have something to share. Share it.

Facebook is the #7th highest ranked Web site on the Internet for web traffic. To put that number in prospective Amazon is ranked #33. Think about that a moment. Authors spend countless hours and sometimes thousands of dollars to get a few copies on a shelf, spine out, in a bookstore visited by a few thousand people per month, in hopes of selling books. Facebook has tens of millions of visitors, and it costs nothing but a little bit of your time.

If you are already listed in Facebook, look me up and add me to your friend list. There aren't too many Pramschufers there so it shouldn't be hard to find me. I started a group called Self-Publishing Basics the other day. You are welcome to join that as well. I am not 100% sure what I am going to do with that group yet so you'll certainly be getting in on the ground floor. If you haven't signed up yet, go do it now. Once you are in, spend some time there and work on your contact page. This is how people will get to know you. There are dozens of modules that can be added to your site to help people get to know you and help you communicate with others. Have some fun, meet some prospects, shake some hands, and sell some books.

Distribution & Marketing Questions

Should I try to get a trade book distributor?

I would at least try to get a distributor for your book. Note: I said "try." Don't get discouraged if you initially come up empty on this one. A distributor will take a 60–75% discount off the retail price to get your book placed in the various wholesale and retail databases so that it is available to the bookstore buyers. Many small publishers put way too much emphasis on this part of the process. Getting a distributor does not guarantee you any actual sales. It does make it easier, however, when you get enough publicity to create a demand for your book. A true distributor works on a commission based on the total sales of the book. In other words, the distributor is not making money unless you are. Beware of those who say they want to distribute your book but want you to pay $500–$1,500 to get you "set up."

My personal favorite used to be a place called Biblio Distributors. They were established for the sole purpose of distributing books for the small press publisher. Their parent company was a huge mainline distributor. Their startup fees were low, and their monthly storage rates were quite reasonable. They were not interested in books printed digitally, which meant you probably need to print at least five hundred to one thousand copies. They were also not interested in your book if you are not the ISBN owner. (And if you are still considering letting someone assign you one of their ISBNs at this stage, you should see a psychiatrist.) In short, they were perfect for the small, yet serious, self-publisher. That's the good news. The bad news is they are now closed. The experiment didn't work, and they left a wake of bad feeling behind. It's a shame because it was a great idea that I thought would work.

There are a few book distributors around who will work with small publishers, but none that I would feel comfortable recommending. I will talk about what I do recommend in a later question.

The next few questions about bookstore distribution had pertained specifically to Biblio but I am leaving it in this fourth edition of the Publishing Basics book because it is good advice, no matter whether you decide to go the traditional bookstore distribution direction or not.

What can I do to qualify to be distributed by a trade distributor?

All distributors have some variation of a review committee set up to decide which books to take and which one to pass. Most will accept only about 10–15% of the submissions they receive; the rest are sent a letter and an evaluation form explaining why they decided not to offer a contract. Overall the goal is to offer contracts only to small presses that they believe publish books they can sell through retail and online bookstores.

Here are the primary reasons for declining a book:

Market: The trade market is very competitive, and they feel that your publishing company is not quite ready or that the market is flooded with similar titles. *Note:* Fiction; poetry; business and economics; self-help; and children's books are particularly hard to sell in the trade market because these categories are so heavily published.

Not right for the trade market: Your title may be better suited for special sales, or the academic and library market. You might consider selling through religious bookstores, direct mail, lectures and seminars, regional bookstores, and online retailers to best reach your audience. You might consider working with a library and/or academic distributor.

Basic book requirements not met (e.g., no ISBN, no bar code, no price on book, price too high, price too low): The price on your book must be competitive for your category, page count, and format. The major accounts are very price-sensitive and the competition is fierce.

Marketing and promotion: The book does not appear to be supported via advertising, marketing, or promotion. Books do not sell just by being on the bookstore shelf or through "word of mouth" alone.

They must have a solid promotion planned in advance of any sales efforts or publication. In addition, Web-based promotion is rarely effective for the trade market. Special sales or back-of-the-room sales do not influence the trade market.

Design: The production value of your book is not competitive with other books in the category. With the vast quantity of books published every year, packaging is the key to sales. Design elements include the typeface, jacket, layout, photo reproduction, table of contents, index, and other features. A spine with the title is essential for placement on store shelves.

Limited subject matter (e.g., poetry or the self-publisher's memoir): Poetry and personal memoirs are very difficult to sell. The audience is extremely limited. Your best options are online retailers and your local bookstore.

Rights/publisher: The applicant is not the owner of the book or ISBN prefix; Xlibris, Lightning Source, or some other such organization is the publisher. Publishers must apply for distribution, not authors.

Future publishing plans: There is no indication of future publishing plans, and the title submitted is not strong enough on its own to support full distribution efforts. *Or* future plans are not focused enough to build a program upon; the publisher should choose a niche market on which to focus its efforts.

Appears to be POD: This rule has more to do with your commitment to your title, as a publisher, than it does to the appearance of a digitally printed book. Distributors are in business to make money and they want only serious publisher/partners. It's hard to convince them you are serious if your total inventory is a digital file on a server somewhere.

What can I do if I can't find a distributor to distribute my book to the trade?

Most of you decided to self-publish because your manuscript was rejected by one, two, five, or one hundred traditional publishers. Being rejected by a distributor at this point is no big deal. After a moment or two of silence, you should head full speed into Plan B. Remember earlier in the book when we talked about POD (print on demand)? How about the final reason listed above for rejecting a book for trade distribution? Now that we have told you everything bad about POD, let me tell you one good thing about it. Back in the early 1990s, Ingram Book Group, one of the world's largest book wholesalers, announced that they were no longer dealing directly with small publishers. If a small publisher wanted to be carried by Ingram, they either needed to be picked up by a distributor or use the POD printing company Ingram owned, Lightning Source. Lightning Source is one of the very few true POD (one at a time) printers in the country. They can afford to be a one-at-a-time printer because their plant is three blocks away from Ingram's main warehouse, making shipping minimal. Lightning Source is tied into a distribution network that includes Ingram, Baker & Taylor, Amazon, and Barnes & Noble.

Here's how it works: In the case of a book ordered on Amazon, the consumer places the order at Amazon. The order is then sent electronically to Lightning Source or other POD printer, which prints and ships the books within twenty-four hours. The publisher is then paid the difference between the wholesale price and the cost of the POD printing. Pretty neat, huh?

In an effort to make something good even better, Self Publishing, Inc., the owner of *SelfPublishing.com*, made a deal with Lightning Source to offer their service at a discount to *SelfPublishing.com* customers—thus the creation of their exclusive Thor Distribution program. The advantage of using the Thor program rather than working with Lightning Source directly is threefold. The start up costs are deferred and subtracted from actual sales rather than paid up front by the author. Second, you get your money quicker. Lightning Source pays publishers ninety days after the end of the month of the sale. Thor pays publishers quarterly on all sales made during the previous quarter. (So for a book sold on March 2, Lightning Source pays the publisher on July 1. With Thor, the publisher would be paid on April 15.) Third, and perhaps most important, Thor looks at POD distribution as a program that is meant to be outgrown. It is an easy, inexpensive way to get your book listed in all the book wholesalers' and retailers' databases so that it will be available at pretty much every store in the country. Please note that I said "available." There is a huge difference between a book being on the bookshelf and a book being available for order, but it's a start. It will give you time to establish the market that was possibly missing the first time you presented your book to a distributor. In my *wbjbradio.com* interview with Davida Breier, formerly from Biblio, she reinforced the idea that Thor is the perfect alternative to traditional distribution, and has no problem picking up a book once the publisher can prove that demand for the title exists based on the POD sales.

Who is Thor?

In Norse mythology Thor was the personification of thunder and the principal war god. Son of the chief god, Odin, and second only to him in importance, Thor was particularly popular among the lower classes of society. He was armed with a hammer (Mjolnir) that returned to his hand after he hurled it at enemies, a belt that doubled his strength when he wore it, and iron gloves that helped him use the Mjolnir effectively. Most of his battles were fought against giants, and he was benevolent to humankind. Thor was noted for his ability to drink vast amounts; he is generally portrayed as a crude, red-bearded, middle-aged warrior who relied on his immense strength rather than on his wits.

According to one popular legend, the giant who constructed the residence of the gods was rewarded with the Mjolnir. When it fell into the giant Thrym's possession, Thor retrieved it by pretending to be the goddess Freya, whom Thrym demanded as his wife in exchange for the hammer.

Thor, also known as Atli, is identified with Donar, the thunder god of Teutonic mythology. His name survives in the English weekday name Thursday, its German counterpart, Donnerstag and in the Dutch Donderdag.

What is Thor Distribution?

Thor Distribution is a strategic alliance between Self Publishing, Inc., a New York printing services company (and the owner of *SelfPublishing.com*) with over 100 million books in print, and Lightning Source, a Tennessee based digital printer owned by book wholesaler giant Ingram. The Thor program provides publishers with a cost effective POD alternative to traditional book distributors.

What is POD?

The meaning of POD (Print on demand) is a printing process where books are printed on an as needed basis, one book at a time. POD has evolved to mean any type of short run printing. There are very few true print on demand printers in America. Lightning Source, RJ Communication's affiliate in Thor Distribution, is the oldest and largest.

What are the benefits of the Thor Distribution Program?

- Cost-effective way to make your books available to the major book wholesalers
- Maximum return for minimum investment
- No inventory sitting in distributors warehouse, unsold but inaccessible to you, the publisher
- Books are printed one at a time, and are only printed if they are sold.
- Books are sold on a non-returnable guarantee sale basis.
- There are no collections or bad debt to worry about.
- Easily converted to traditional distributor

What are the disadvantages of the Thor Distribution program?

There is only one real disadvantage to the program. That is while your book is available to over 90% of the bookstores in the US; they are not physically on the shelves of any bookstore. This is balanced by the fact that the Independent Publisher is required to print at least one hundred books (five hundred minimum is preferred) before they can be a part of Thor Distribution. It is these books that are the "seeds" for the buzz that the publisher is going to create for their book.

How do I get started?

It's easy to get started. The first thing you need to do is fill out the marketing submission form. Once you have printed at least one hundred copies of your book through *SelfPublishing.com*, you sign up for the Thor program. As soon as your initial order of books is completed to your satisfaction, your digital file will be uploaded for POD distribution. It's as easy as that.

How much does it cost to have my book distributed by Thor Distributors?

In addition to whatever is spent for your initial printing of books through *SelfPublishing.com*, the basic cost of the program is $249 for three years. No "up front" money is needed. The $249 will be subtracted from your quarterly earnings until it is paid.

How much money will I make per book sold through Thor Distributors?

You make the difference between the wholesale cost and the cost of printing. The wholesale cost is 50% of the retail cost, and you set the retail cost, so you control how much you make. Realistically, you need to set the retail price of your book to be in line with other similar books in a bookstore. Take a walk through your local bookstore to get a feel for the best retail price for your book. For figuring purposes, we'll assume that your book is 256 pages and will retail for $14.95. Your wholesale price is $7.50. Your printing price for wholesale sales is figured at $.013 per page plus $.90/book or $4.23, so your profit will be $3.25 per book. That $3.25 remains the same no matter how few or how many books are sold through this POD method. The best thing about this number is that it is a net number so there are no other costs to be subtracted.

NOTE: These prices are the actual costs at Lightning Source at the time of this printing. They are subject to change at any time. Double check the *SelfPublishing.com* Web site for current pricing prior to signing up.

When do I get paid?

Checks are sent out quarterly for both *JustBookz.com* bookstore sales as well as Thor POD sales.

Can I have my book printed somewhere else and still participate in the Thor Distribution Program?

Sorry but this program is strictly reserved for customers of Self Publishing, Inc., (*BooksJustBooks.com, SelfPublishing.com, RJcom.com*).

Does Thor have an online bookstore to help me sell my book?

Yes. The Self Publishing, Inc., bookstore is located at *JustBookz.com*. Like the Thor Distribution Program, *JustBookz.com* is reserved exclusively for customers of Self Publishing, Inc.. Books sold through *JustBookz.com* are sold at a 40% discount, compared to the Thor program's 50%. Publishers may also request a "buy me" button that can be placed on their Web site, enabling their visitors to buy books from their Web site but have the actual order handled by Self Publishing, Inc..

Who controls the retail price of my book?

You do! It's as easy as that. Along with all the other Vanity Press negatives, many of them control the retail cost and price your book so high that nobody but the author would ever buy it. (Oh, but that's their idea, remember?)

Why do I have to buy at least one hundred copies of my book before I can participate in the Thor Distribution program?

One hundred is the minimum number of copies needed to get started with Thor. *SelfPublishing.com* wants authors who are serious about marketing their book. Between friends and family, a couple of review copies and maybe a local bookstore signing or two, one hundred copies probably won't last very long. Remember, it's not going to be easy marketing a book. Don't stack the deck against yourself by not having a physical book to show.

Why can't I have my full color children's book in Thor?

While the pricing for digital printing has come down in the past few years, it is still not low enough to work efficiently at 50% of the retail price. Some of the POD vanity presses have convinced many authors that POD works— but it doesn't, at least not beyond sales to the author. Do I think that this will change? Absolutely, just like it did with black & white. Just not yet. Keep an eye on the Children's Book section of *SelfPublishing.com* for updates. You can bet as soon as it makes sense to offer color POD, we will—but not a moment sooner.

Why do you recommend that I make an initial order of at least five hundred copies of my trade book?

If you have researched independent self-publishing much at all, you have probably run across Dan Poynter. His "New Book Model" calls for three hundred to five hundred copies as a start. We say five hundred copies because that is where *SelfPublishing.com* starts printing using a traditional offset printing press, whereas fewer than five hundred copies are printed on a digital press. Actually, for very few dollars more, you can buy seven hundred-fifty copies. There is one thing I know for sure; if you think you can sell five hundred books, I can pretty much guarantee that you'll sell seven hundred-fifty or a thousand or more. If you do not have an idea of where you'll sell the first book—stick with an initial order of one hundred.

What is the difference between the Thor Program and other POD programs?

The idea of POD was originally developed to allow large publishers an opportunity to keep their backlist alive indefinitely after the titles had run their course through the system. Instead of having to reprint a couple thousand books to keep a title in print, a publisher only needed to have a digital copy on file at a POD printer so books could be ordered on an as needed basis. This is still the primary use of POD.

The Vanity Press publishers jumped on the POD idea as a method to limit their printing expense while maximizing the profits made off their authors. Vanity Press publishers sell very few books to anyone but the author and the author's friends and family. They make most of their money from up front costs to their customers. The last thing that the Vanity Publisher needs is inventory because they aren't going to sell any books anyway.

Thor Distribution looks at POD as a starting point for a new title in the bookstore sales process. It is meant to serve as a "place saver" for the publisher until bookstore sales get to the point where it pays to have a book distributed through a traditional book distributor. Bookstore income is treated as "found money" while the publisher devotes time and effort into obtaining publicity and selling inventory copies into the special sales market. That is why the Thor distribution is only offered as an add-on to a regular print run (minimum one hundred copies— suggested at least five hundred copies).

Can I sell books directly to bookstores, or is this an exclusive distribution arrangement?

Yes! Please do. The beauty of the Thor Distribution program is that the publisher is free to sell to any retailer they can. Some bookstores have exclusive arrangements with Ingram or Baker & Taylor, so sales to them would come through Thor, but most do not. If you arrange a book signing at a local bookstore, you are free to sell books out of your inventory at whatever price you wish. You are also free to pursue any retail chain you'd like. The idea behind the program is to free the publisher of the worry about getting their book listed in the major wholesale databases so marketing efforts can be focused on narrower and more manageable targets initially.

Is Thor Distribution meant to take the place of traditional distributors?

No! The Thor distribution program is designed to serve as a starting point.

Most independent publishers lack the funds to effectively market a book to the national market. Getting a new book into the marketplaces is normally a slow process. The math really doesn't work using a traditional distributor unless you can guarantee a couple thousand bookstore copies per year. This is only going to happen after the publisher builds a demand for a book. Once the bookstore sales are there using the POD method, a traditional distributor can take it to the next level.

Sample Book

- 6 x 9", perfect bound
- 256 pages plus cover
- 50# white offset
- 4 color laminated cover
- $14.95 retail

Copies Sold	rjcom.com unit cost per copy*	Your gross profit/copy for sales via distributor @ 60% discount**	Thor unit cost per copy***	Your net profit /copy on all sales
500 copies	$5.42	$.056	$4.23	$3.25
750 copies	$3.90	$.2.08	$4.23	$3.25
1000 copies	$3.16	$2.82	$4.23	$3.25
1500 copies	$2.38	$3.60	$4.23	$3.25
2000 copies	$2.00	$3.98	$4.23	$3.25
3000 copies	$1.59	$4.39	$4.23	$3.25

*plus shipping and all copies printed at same time
** Not included is any freight to and from, returns, restocking fees, storage all which publisher pays
*** Thor copies print one at a time

How many books do I need to sell through book wholesalers to make it financially viable to use a traditional distributor?

The chart opposite shows you the dollars and cents comparison between the two types of distribution. It will give you an idea of where you need to be to start considering a traditional distributor.

How long will it take to outgrow the Thor Distribution Program?

You are never more that one phone call away from outgrowing the Thor program. By removing the worry of bookstore distribution, the publisher's full attention can be devoted to promoting the book. A couple of good reviews, a couple of interviews could easily get book sales to the level needed to make dealing with a traditional distributor worthwhile. On the other hand, a book may never outgrow the Thor Program. Several hundred copies or fewer per year may sell through brick and mortar bookstores, but remember—it's found money, so that's not bad either.

If I use the Thor POD distribution system, why do I also need to buy a regular press run of books?

The answer to this is simple. First off, even on a good day, only about 25% of the total books you sell will be to bookstores; the other 75% will be sold to alternative markets. It is these alternative markets where the author/publisher has the best chance of being successful through his or her own efforts. Real books are needed for this. You also need real books for promotion and to send out for review. Also, you will most likely need printed books if you are going to do any in-store book signings. Bookstores don't normally want to order non-returnable books, which is the form in which POD books are sold. In short, POD distribution is merely a starting point. It is not as good as being carried by a traditional distributor, but it is infinitely better than having no outlet at all.

In what other ways do you suggest I market my book?

There is no limit to marketing ideas for your books. What works for you, doesn't necessarily work for someone else. Keep this in mind when you are looking at marketing ideas. Personally, I have not seen a single marketing idea worth more than $500. Here are a few ideas that fall well under that number.

1001 Ways to Market Your Book

The first thing you need to do is visit *JustBookz.com* and buy a discounted copy of John Kremer's *1001 Ways to Market Your Book*. It's been around for a while and some of the statistical data is a little dated, but you can't go wrong picking up a copy. I guarantee you will pick up a few tips that will be more than worth your while and help you sell books.

Press Release

A good press release is a little like a good cover design. The *SelfPublishing.com* people lean toward the lower-priced, higher-quality companies. *SelfPublishing.com* works closely with an agency located at *Send2Press.com*. There are a wide range of services available. The one thing I would highly recommend is to have them edit your press release or even write it for you. It's an affordable expense that will significantly increase the odds of getting people in the media to react to your release. Be realistic, though, in what you expect from a press release. For the most part, reporters aren't sitting there just waiting for you to come along so they can interview you and give you free publicity. One good by-product of sending out a press release is that even if you do not get any calls from the press, your press release will appear on hundreds of Web sites all over the Internet. Make sure you have your Web site linked to your press release. You never know who will click through and take a look.

JustBookz.com Online Bookstore

Started in late 2002, the *JustBookz.com* online bookstore was created to provide an affordable alternative to *Amazon.com* and *Barnes&Noble.com*. All *SelfPublishing.com* customers are eligible to be included in the store. There are no setup fees, and they charge only 40% of the retail price on sales, compared with the 55% charged by Amazon and B&N. Internet keyword marketing is also performed, at no cost to the author/publisher, if the book lends itself to this type of marketing. The theme of this bookstore is that Tom Clancy doesn't need any more of your money. Buy independent.

Special-Sales Marketing

My friend Brian Jud, a well-known marketing guru for small press publishers, has developed several tools to help guide you to non-bookstore markets in which to sell your book.

First is the Special-Sales Profit Center™, a Web-based, prospect-rich, targeted marketing system that helps deliver incremental sales and profits to you. The Profit Center is an online contact management system that gives you a continuing supply of sales leads customized for each of your titles. It can increase your productivity by organizing the process of contacting prospects and converting them to customers. The Profit Center can improve your profitability by directing your sales efforts to those most likely to buy your titles. Since it is Web-based, it permits access from remote locations so you can have the information you need wherever you are.

Second is Brian's book *Beyond the Bookstore*, a Publishers Weekly selection that shows you how to sell your books to non-bookstore markets, more profitably and with no returns. There are seventy-nine strategies in *Beyond the Bookstore* that show you how to tap the enormous, lucrative market of special sales. You will discover the secrets of selling more of your books in new places, increasing sales and profits as you minimize returns, and contacting buyers successfully.

Beyond the Bookstore contains the *Marketing Planning* CDROM™, with templates for planning and tracking sales and expenses. This CD-ROM walks you through the steps for creating a customized marketing plan. It helps you increase profits by offering practical marketing help.

Learn to Expertize

Another thing I'd highly recommend you do, if you want more attention for your book from major magazines, newspapers, and talk shows, is learn something about Fern Reiss's *Expertizing*. Fern has been quoted, and her books mentioned, in over one hundred publications, from the *New York Times* and the *Wall Street Journal* to *Fortune Small Business* and *Wall Street Week* to *USA Today* and *Glamour*. *Expertizing* is about getting more media attention for your book and business, and Fern has *Expertized* small businesses, large businesses, and non-profits—everyone from the Hilton Hotels Corporation to the United Methodist Church. Most of her *Expertizing* techniques work particularly well for authors and independent publishers.

One example of what you'll learn in *Expertizing* is how to generate irresistible media sound bites. A few years back, Fern wanted to get some media attention for her book, *Terrorism and Kids: Comforting Your Child*. She noticed that a Voice of America reporter was doing a story, and since Voice of America broadcasts to an international audience, she thought it might be a good way to get foreign sales. The problem was, the journalist wasn't doing a piece on terrorism. He was doing a story on the sudden popularity of home theatre systems. But Fern managed to get an astounding fifteen minutes on Voice of America, in his piece on home theater systems, for her book on terrorism and children. Here's what she emailed the journalist:

> "You can thank Osama bin Laden for the sudden popularity of home theatre systems. Americans, post 9/11, are bringing their entertainment into their homes; it's a 9/11 nesting response. And I'm the author of a book, *Terrorism and Kids: Comforting Your Child...*"

Fern says that once you learn this sort of technique, you can get into any publication—with any book—on any topic! Her all-day *Expertizing* workshops happen at the Ritz Carlton Hotels in Boston, New York, and San Francisco, or you can sign up for her free monthly *Expertizing* email newsletter.

Online Radio Showcases

I started a Podcast, which is a fancy word for online radio show, during the summer of 2005. My show is titled Publishing Basics Radio, where weekly we help you navigate the self-publishing mine-field. Audio on the Internet is something that I have toyed with for the past couple years. The availability of cable and DSL connections that are affordable to just about anyone, in combination with the explo-sion of Apple's iPod, has made online audio a reality. Errol Smith, a pioneer of the Readers Radio Network, and Allan Hunkin, the owner of *Podcast.com*, are two of the leaders in this field, and both have pro-grams of special interest to publishers.

Readers Radio has a network of over ten thousand Web sites that have agreed to sell books within the site's particular specialty. With Readers Radio, you are interviewed by Emmy award winner Errol Smith about your book. This interview is edited and then posted on sites within the Readers Radio Network, as well as on sites researched by the author. For this service, Readers Radio is paid a reasonable fee, plus a percentage of the sales of all books sold though the network. Allan Hunkin has a similar program, where the author is interviewed, for a reasonable fee, and then is given the interview outright to use in marketing his or her books. Both programs are good and afford-able. You can find out more information about these programs at *SelfPublishing.com*.

Trade Shows

Trade shows are a good way of getting your book in front of many retail book buyers. Unfortunately, they are quite expensive for a one- or two-book publisher and are rarely the "pot of gold at the end of the rainbow" that all newcomers envision them to be. Your best bet is to ease into these shows. The largest show in the United States is the annual Book Expo America. This show generally moves between New York, Chicago, and Los Angeles. The least expensive way to participate in this, as well as many regional shows, is to join Independent Book Publishers Association (ibpa) and take part in one of their co-op programs.

Trade Associations

I purposely left trade associations for last. There are many different trade associations that cater to the small press customer. Unfortunately, very few (if any) of these organizations want a press that is too small (like author/publishers with a single title). They will all let you join and have nice newsletters, but keep in mind that most of the information they provide and the services they offer are really meant for the larger independent publisher. Personally, I feel that there is a need for a trade association specifically geared to the one- and two-title publisher. After your third or fourth title, you graduate to one of the other associations. Maybe Self Publishing, Inc., will start such an association one day. For now you're on your own. The two main small press associations are Independent Book Publishers Association and Small Press Association of North America (SPAN).

Remember, your book is not going to sell itself. The only way that there will be demand for your book is if you help create that demand. Luck replaces hard work only in very rare circumstances.

Are there ways to be sure I make money on my book?

I believe you can find ways if you put your mind to it. I have been fortunate enough to do so with one of my self-published books, *Soups and Stories from the Realm of Queen Arnold*. Dick Elms, a retired printer and proofreader, and a neighbor of mine, had fifty fabulous soup recipes he wanted to publish. That didn't seem to be enough for a book. As Penrod Waterman, I had published eight short stories over the years, but that was not enough to carry a book either. So we invented the great queen and her mythical realm.

Queen Arnold, as it turns out, arrived on Broadneck (a peninsula just north of Annapolis, Maryland, on Chesapeake Bay) from England on the seventh day of the seventh month of the 777th year with her party of 777 men, women, and children. Known for her enthralling sensual magnetism, her exuberant mirth, her extraordinary vivacity, her flawless beauty, her blunt rusticity, and her kiss-provoking lips, Queen Arnold ruled over an ideal realm for seventy-seven years. Back then, the Arnoldites ate soup just before darkness oozed around the forest; then, as delicately emerging stars and small campfires magnified the subduing charm of the woods, peerless raconteurs began to amuse and enchant young and old alike with fabulous stories.

I made sure the book made money by pre-selling eight hundred copies. In exchange for suggesting their wines as appropriate accompaniments to each of the fifty soup recipes, a group of affiliated wineries bought four hundred of the books at just below the retail price. We dedicated the book to the memory of a great soup-making grandmother whose family still owned a local wine and spirits shop. They bought two hundred copies to sell in their store. Then, in the acknowledgments, we touted a local tree service as being the most environmentally concerned and historically sensitive in the world. They bought two hundred copies from us to give to their preferred customers in the Arnold area.

Not every book lends itself to these kinds of sales, but perhaps this example will inspire you to think of some prepublication connections you can make.

Will I be able to get my book on Oprah?

It's possible, but there are five conditions. First, you have to catch a weasel when it's asleep. Second, you have to make a silk purse out of a pig's ear. Third, you must extract sunbeams from cucumbers. Fourth, Elvis Presley must receive a posthumous best actor award for his portrayal of Jess Wade in *Charro*. And fifth, Mongolia must become the fifty-first state.

The point: Stay realistic. Work hard at marketing day by day. Wasn't it Edison who said, "Success is 1% inspiration and 99% perspiration"?

PHOTO SECTION

The following pages show examples of different types of artwork and photos. Note: This book was printed on offset equipment and is a sample of that process (books with print runs of 500 or more). For samples printed on digital equipment (for similar books with print runs of under 500 copies) contact your book coach or Ron@rjcom.com.

Helvetica thin	12 on 18 leading	15% black background
Helvetica thin	12 on 18 leading	no background
Helvetica	12 on 18 leading	30% black background
Helvetica	12 on 18 leading	no background
Helvetica medium	12 on 18 leading	60% black background
Helvetica medium	12 on 18 leading	no background
Helvetica black	12 on 18 leading	75% black background
Helvetica black	12 on 18 leading	no background
Helvetica black	12 on 18 leading	100% black background

Publishing Basics

Chapter 23

Chapter 24

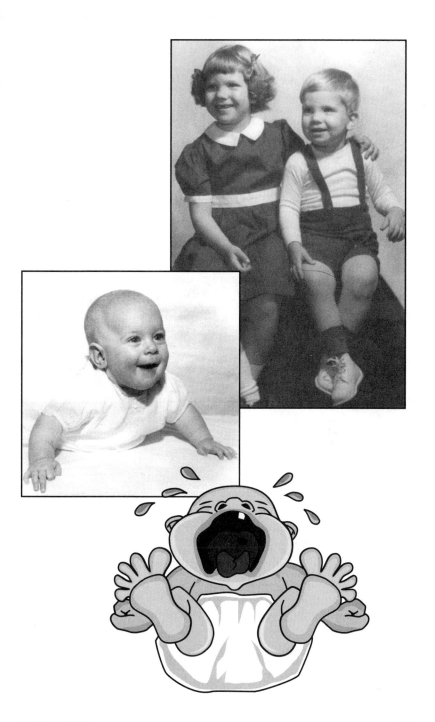

INDEX

Do I need an index for my book?

Generally, non-fiction books have indexes. Like everything else in publishing, indexes run a range from quite simple to complex with corresponding pricing. The two basic types are ones prepared by computer and ones prepared by hand. Rather then talking about it, I thought I would take the space in this book to show you the difference so you can make the choice of which type fits your needs and budget.

The first example is a **software-generated index**. This type of index starts with a list of proper nouns and capitalized words generated from the final layout. The author then chooses which words to index, deletes all the rest, and sends the list back to the designer. The designer then runs the edited list back through the software and the index is created and added to the back of the book. From the first draft the author may make adjustments. Part of the initial word list for the Publishing Basics book and the resulting index follows.

The second example is a **hand-constructed index**. This type of index is done the old-fashioned way—a person with a good eye and a huge stack of index cards works diligently through your layout and decides what needs to be indexed. This often includes many more entries than the software-generated index.

If the software-generated index is sufficient for your needs, it costs about $100 above the cost of your basic text layout. If you prefer the hand-constructed index, you need to figure about $4/page. You be the judge… it's your choice.

Examples of the list of proper nouns and capitalized words from the final layout. This is the first step in the software-generated index process.

Acknowledgments
Acrobat Reader
Additional Proofing Pass
Advanced Reader Copies
Advertising
Allan Hunkin
Alternative Offset
Amazon
Animal House
Annapolis
ANSI
AOL
Apostrophes
Apple
April
ARC
Arial
Art
Arthur Plotnik
ASCII
ASP
Atli
Audio
Author
Baker
Barnes
BarnesandNoble
Bias
Biblio
Bill Gates
BISAC
Bleed
Bob Johnson Publishing
Book Expo America
Book Industry Standards
Book Industry Study Group
Book Industry Subject
Bookland
BooksJustBooks
Bookstore
Bookstores
Boston
Bound Galleys
Bowker
Bowker Web
BoyBrenda Ueland
Brian Jud
Broadneck Baloney
Broadneck Hundred
Buy

Buyer Beware
Buzz
Casewraps
Category
CD
Century Schoolbook
Chapbook
Charro
Check
Chesapeake Bay
Chicago Tribune
Child
CHILDREN
CMYK
Colons
Commas
Common

International Standard Book Number
Internet
ISBN Agency
ISBNs
Isn
Jackets
Jess Wade
Jim Salisbury
John Kremer
JustBookz
Kathleen Krull
Keyboard Viewer
Kindle
Kinko
Lay-Flat
Layout
LCCN
Library of Congress
Lightning Source
Linda
Linotype
Los Angeles
Mac
Made
Mailboxes
MANUFACTURING QUESTIONS
Market Your Book
Marketing
Marketing Planning CDROM
Marketing Questions
Mechanical
Mechanical Edit
Mechanical Editing
Mechanical Editing
Menu Bar
Microsoft Word
Moisture
MS Publisher
MS Word
New York City
New York Times
North American ISBN
Note
Notes
Num Lock
Offset
On-demand
Online Bookstore

Editing
Editor
Editorial Analysis
EDITORIAL QUESTIONS
Elements of Editing
Ellipses
Elvis Presley
Emmy
Errol Smith
Erwin Knoll
European Article Number
Facebook
FAQs
FedEx Ground
Fern Reiss
Fiction
Flaps

Online Radio Showcases
Oops
Oprah
Ota-Bind
Overseas Printing
PageMaker
Pantone
Paris Review
Parthenon
PDF
Penrod Waterman
Permissions
Photoshop
Pine Tree Boulevard
PMA
PMS
Portable Document Format
Pramschufer
Pre-Assigned Card Catalog Number
Press Release
Printing Trade Customs
Production Center
Profit Center
PTA
Publishers Directory
Publishers Marketing Association
Publishers Weekly
PUBLISHING BASICS
Publishing Basics Newsletter
Publishing Basics Radio
Quark
Quotation
R.R. Bowker
Radio
Random House
Readers Radio
Readers Radio Network
Repro
Review Copy
Review Purposes Only
Ritz Carlton Hotels
RJ Communication
Robert Bowie Johnson
Robie Macauley
Ron Pramschufer
Royalties
Saddle
Sample Book

Sample Comprehensive Edit
San Francisco
Self-publisher
Self-Publishing Basics
Selfpublishing
Semicolon
Send2Press
SEO
Serif
Shipping
Short-run
Short-Run Offset
Show Input Menu
Single ISBN
Small Press
Small Press Association of North America
Small Press Record of Books
Solving Light Books
Special-Sales Marketing
Special-Sales Profit Center
Substantive Edit
Substantive Editing
Suitcase
Thor Distribution
Thor Distribution Program
Thor Distributors
Thor POD
Thor Program
Times New Roman
Tom Clancy
Traditional Sheetfed Printing
Unedited Galleys
UPS
URL
US Copyright Office
US Customs Service
Vanity Press
Vanity Press Publishers
Voice of America
Wall Street Journal
Wall Street Week
Web Offset
Web Site Development
Web Site Marketing
WEB SITE QUESTIONS
Web-based
WordPerfect
Xerox
Xlibris

Software-Generated Index

SEO (Search Engine Optimization), 77

Shipping, 61, 84

Short-run, 2, 35, 45-46, 50-52

Short-Run Offset, 51

Single ISBN, 16

Small Press Association of North America, 98

Special-Sales Marketing, 95

Substantive Editing, 27

Thor Distribution, 84, 86-91, 93

Thor POD, 84, 88, 93

Times New Roman, 29

Traditional Sheetfed Printing, 51-52, 72

Unedited Galleys, 44

UPS, 7, 61

URL, 7, 76

US Copyright Office, 12

US Customs Service, 13

Vanity Press, 4, 8, 10, 16, 89-90

Web Offset, 52

Web Site Development, 73

Web Site Marketing, 76

Web Site Questions, 73

Hand-Constructed Index

proofs of, 55

dedication pages, vii
design issues
    book covers, 34, 35–38
    hybrid covers, 35
    hybrid text design, 35
    margins, 28
    spine width, 36–37
    text preparation, 30–34
    typeface, 28
digital printing
    compared to offset, 40–44
    explained, 50–51
distribution
    costs of, 87–88, 92–93
    Lightning Source, 84–85
    and print on demand, 84–85
    process of, 81–85
    Thor, 84–85, 86–94
domain names, 73–74

editing, 19–27
Editorial Analysis, 20–21, 23–27
endleaves, 58, 67
e-publishing, 11–12
expenses
    color, 54
    distribution, 87–88, 92–93
    printing, 47, 53, 60–62, 92
    reprinting, 62
    shipping, 61
    web sites, 75, 76
expertise as marketing tool, 96–97
Expertizing (Reiss), 96–97

Facebook as marketing tool, 78–80
fonts, 28, 102
foreign printers, 46, 70–71
four-color process, 53

galley proofs. *See* proofs
grain, paper, 42–43

hard copy, 32
hardcover bindings, 57, 68
hybrid covers, 35
hybrid text design, 35

ibpa (Independent Book Publishers
    Association), 98
illustrations. *See also* artwork, original
    children's books, 65–66
    examples, 102–106
Independent Book Publishers
    Association (ibpa), 98
indexes
    examples, 108–110
    types of, 107
Ingram Book Group, 84–85
ISBN (International Standard Book
    Number)
    assignment of, 4, 7, 15–17
    example, ii
    functions of, 15–18

jackets. *See* covers
Jud, Brian, 95–96
JustBookz.com, 88–89, 95

Kindle readers, 12

LCCN (Library of Congress Catalog
    Number)
    assignment of, 7, 18
    example, ii
legal issues in printing, 59
length of books, 64
Library of Congress Catalog Number.
    See LCCN
Lightning Source, 84–85, 86

magazines for writers, 20
margins, 28
marketing
    with Facebook, 78–80

What They Say

SelfPublishing.com, BooksJustBooks.com and RJcom.com are all Web sites of Self Publishing, Inc. These comments may have come from any one of these sites, but all reflect the level of our customer service.

"Your site and staff are fantastic! They had answers for every question, addressed every issue I had and solved any problem that came up. I had a certain vision for my book and they understood that every step of the way and did everything to make sure that my vision became a reality. The final outcome was even better than I had expected!"
—Emoni Haydes, *Quest for Solitude*

"At the beginning, I was unsure whether to go with you. I liked Ron and was leaning that way. Then I spoke for two hours with Sana Shabazz—she had published with them herself. She spoke in glowing terms of their service. That convinced me. I found the staff personable and responsive. The book design was beautiful and the layout really sharp-looking. I would highly recommend them to anybody looking to self-publish."
—Author of *Husky Football in the Don James Era*

"Wish I had SOMETHING to complain about as I've run out of superlatives on your wonderful staff and how comprehensive the help was in guiding us from conception to delivery. We have used BJB services twice now, and both times the process was exceptionally easy. The final product was everything we has hoped for. Quality was paramount as this was a religious publication for regular use, paid for by members. We had unanimous approval by all who contributed. Our thanks to all!"
—Author of *Psalms and Selected Scriptures*

"Aside from the book's topic, a major reason why my self-published book sold so well—it's now in its fourth printing!—is that it was professionally designed and printed by Books Just Books."
—Author of *Our Town, Our Time*

"I have used *www.booksjustbooks.com* as an information resource as well as printing avenue for both editions of my non-fiction title. The service and response have been outstanding."
—Linda VandeVrede, *Press Releases are not a PR Strategy*

"I highly recommend self-publishers take advantage of the excellent services provided by RJ Communications."
—Leon M. Kelly, *Confessions of a So-Called Sex Offender*

"Everyone was more than positive and professional and if ever I know of someone who needs a place to print books of any sort I'll tell them of you. People were very helpful and not too prissy, just right on all sorts of levels, I wish you all great raises for this year."
—Author of *Wake Up America*

"The folks at Self Publishing I believe are the best in the business. There are no surprises, everything is laid out for you, even for the novice. Folks like me publishing their first book and others that may be on their 20th book are treated with respect and given insight into all aspects that are needed to not just get our books published but into the public's hands. I appreciate all their help. From the operator answering your phone call to the very top. Each person treats you as an individual and not just one of the masses. I would highly recommend them to anyone needing to publish."
—Author of *The Fiery Furnace of Cancer*

"The folks at RJCommunications took the fear out of self publishing for me."
—Author of *Death of a Hustler*

"My initial plunge into the self-publishing arena has been very gratifying, and RJ has been extremely helpful as well as supportive. Dana Cole's editorial work was very helpful and reflected a breadth of review and analysis that I hadn't expected but greatly appreciated. Jonathan's work on the design was also well done....love the product (and of course hope readers will too!)."
—Peter Dumas, *Seasons in the Fall*

"I've been recommending your website to anyone interested in self-publishing."
—Author of *Positive Discipline for Parenting in Recovery*

"I hoped for excellent service, and your company over-delivered. I'm recommending you to other people I'm going to start working with. Worked mostly with Jonathan who was great both professionally and personally."
—Arnie Z. Goldberg, *Why Jews Don't Camp, Plus 24 Other Hilarious Stories About Everyday Life*

"Jonathan Gullery and Bob Powers were absolutely the best supporters in this self publishing venture. I can't wait to do it again with my next book!!"
—Author of *The First Lady*

"I really liked working with Ron Pramschufer. He didn't try to sell me anything. Rather he asked questions about my expectations for my book and helped me make good decisions for myself. In doing so, I ordered the right amount of books to meet my needs."
—Author of *Monster Relationships: Taming the Beasts that are Killing Your Relationships*

"Judging from my experience thus far, I would recommend *SelfPublishing.com* to anyone who's interested in learning about the self publishing business. I would also highly recommend your company for the first-time self publisher...like myself."
—Quincella C. Geiger, *Bringing Home the Baking*

"The folks at RJ are absolutely top notch. They have not forgotten what customer service means. Everyone I dealt with was courteous, friendly, eager and willing to help with anything and everything. When I had a question which could not be answered by the person I had on the phone, I was sent directly to Ron. To say that my experience with RJ was anything but STELLAR would be an understatement. Everyone there gets a two thumbs up from this author! Not only will I continue to use RJ, but I will recommend them, with the highest regard, to anyone interested in quality and a professional result."

—Debbie Ramsey, *Eden Moon*

"I was extremely happy with the results. It was easy, efficient and the end product was excellent. I definitely plan to use your services for my next book!"

—Mary Ann Winiger, *A Revolution of One*

"Before reading your *Publishing Basics* I knew nothing about self publishing. It was a wealth of knowledge and I highly recommend it to any new author or first time self publisher"

—Author of *Breaking the Chain of Shame*

"Denise—I want to thank you and the other RJC staff, especially Jonathan, Bob, Jacki, and you, for all that has been done to get *The Wealthy Shepherd*, by Mark Schaffner, into print. All 400 copies of the initial printing were delivered at 7:00 PM yesterday. The shiny new books look great! In fact, when I opened one of the boxes to check the contents, the UPS delivery person was so impressed with the cover and title that he said "Say, I'm interested in that!" and asked if he could get a copy. Again, thanks to all of you for being so helpful. We'll be calling for more of your services soon."

—Glen Robinson

"From the minute I clicked on RJ's website and found *Booksjustbooks*, my experience with this company has been beyond expectations. Every question or issue was resolved quickly and efficiently by the very knowledgeable and competent staff. I will be back to have my next title printed at RJ, and I highly recommend them to anyone who is interested in self-publishing. Certainly, research the other options, and I'm sure you will come to the same conclusion that I have: This is the best place for your printing needs. Kudos to everyone at RJ for a job well done!"

—Author of *Chance Encounter*

"Your staff took my project seriously and made my project their project. Your staff made my work look better than I would have ever been able to do on my own. Your staff's experience and commitment to customer service gave me a great final product."

—Bill Palmer, *To the Colors*

"RJ Communications is one of the few companies that are 100% in the author's corner."

—Mark Levine, *The Fine Print of Self Publishing*

"I cannot praise your company enough. Each member of your company has been extremely effective and professional. All deadlines were met. Costs were reasonable. Any and all individuals interested in writing a book or books would be foolish not to use your services. Ron, I am sure you have a lot to do with how your team works. Congratulations! I thank you very much."

—Bernard Gassaway, *Reflections of an Urban High School Principal*

"As a self-publisher, the service and product provided by your computer was outstanding. I will continue to publish additional books through your company and recommend your company to others. Keep up the outstanding work and service."

—Angel Ramos, *Triumph of the Spirit: The DPN Chronicle*

Seymour S

PLANETS AROUND THE SUN

SeaStar Books · San Francisco

This book is dedicated to my grandson Joel.

Special thanks to reading consultant Dr. Linda B. Gambrell, Director of the School of Education at Clemson University, past president of the National Reading Conference, and past board member of the International Reading Association.

Permission to use the following photographs is gratefully acknowledged: Front cover, title page: Science Photo Library, Photo Researchers, Inc.; pages 2–3, 6–7, 14–17, 26–31: National Space Science Data Center; pages 8–9: The Team Leader, Prof. Bruce C. Murray and National Space Science Data Center; pages 10–11: Dr. Robert W. Carslon, The Galileo Project and National Space Science Data Center; pages 12–13: The Principal Investigator, Dr. Frederick J. Doyle and National Space Science Data Center; pages 18–25: The Team Leader, Dr. Bradford A. Smith and National Space Science Data Center.

ISBN-10: 1-58717-146-5 ISBN-13: 978-1-58717-146-8

SeaStar is an imprint of Chronicle Books LLC.

Library of Congress Cataloging-in-Publication Data is available.

10 9 8 7 6 5

Chronicle Books LLC
680 Second Street, San Francisco, California 94107

www.chroniclekids.com